BELTS AND CHAINS

A basic guide to the maintenance, installation, and failure diagnosis
of belt and chain drives

FUNDAMENTALS OF SERVICE

PUBLISHER
DEERE & COMPANY
JOHN DEERE PUBLISHING
one John Deere Place
Moline, IL 61265
http://www.johndeere.com/publications
1–800–522–7448

Fundamentals of Service (FOS) is a series of manuals created by Deere & Company. Each book in the series is conceived, researched, outlined, edited, and published by Deere & Company, John Deere Publishing. Authors are selected to provide a basic technical manuscript that could be edited and rewritten by staff editors.

HOW TO USE THE MANUAL: This manual can be used by anyone — experienced mechanics, shop trainees, vocational students, and lay readers.

Persons not familiar with the topics discussed in this book should begin with Chapter 1 and then study the chapters in sequence. The experienced person can find what is needed on the "Contents" page.

Each guide was written by Deere & Company, John Deere Publishing staff in cooperation with the technical writers, illustrators, and editors at Almon, Inc. — a full-service technical publications company headquartered in Waukesha, Wisconsin (www.almoninc.com).

FOR MORE INFORMATION: This book is one of many books published on agricultural and related subjects. For more information or to request a FREE CATALOG, call 1–800–522–7448 or send your request to address above or:

**Visit Us on the Internet
http://www.johndeere.com/
publications**

ACKNOWLEDGEMENTS:

John Deere gratefully acknowledges help from the following groups:

For Belts: B.F. Goodrich Co.; Dayco Corp.; Dodge Firestone Industrial Products Co.; Gates Rubber Co.; Goodyear Tire &Rubber Co.; Mechanical Power Transmission Assn.; Standard Oil Co.; Rubber Manufacturers Assn. (RMA); Worthington Corp.

For Chains: Rex Chainbelt Inc.; American Oil Co.; American Society of Agricultural Engineers (ASAE); American Sprocket Chain Manufacturers Assn.; Chain Belt Co.; Diamond Chain Co.; Link-Belt Co.; Ramsay Products Corp.; Society of Automotive Engineers (SAE); Whitney Chain Co.

 JOHN DEERE We have a long-range interest in Vocational Education

CONTENTS

1 *BELTS*

2 *CHAINS*

APPENDIX

BELTS

Introduction

Round belt, flat belt and V-belt drives are **frictional** drives. They transmit rotational force (torque) by contact between the belt and the driving pulley and one or more driven pulleys.

The belt must be designed, manufactured and maintained properly to enable the belt to transfer this torque efficiently and reliably. It should also be designed to slip or break if the upper torque limits are exceeded in order to prevent possible damage to driven components.

The ability of frictional drive belts to transmit power depends on:

- *Tension holding the belt to the pulleys.*
- *Friction between the belt and the pulleys.*
- *Arc of contact (or "wrap") between the belt and the pulleys.*
- *Speed of the belt.*

Belts are normally used to transmit power between two parallel shafts but they are flexible and can also be used in a variety of other ways.

ADVANTAGES OF BELTS (COMPARED WITH CHAINS)

- Belts require no lubrication.
- Belt drives generally operate with less noise.
- Belts are smooth starting and running.
- Belts dampen vibration between the driving and driven machines.
- Belts provide overload protection for the drive system because they will not transmit a severe overload of power, except for a very brief time.
- Flat belt drives can be used where extremely long center distances make chain drives impractical.
- Flat belts are advantageous for extremely high speeds.
- Single belt drives will accept more misalignment than chain drives.
- Many belt drives are less expensive for low horsepower and low ratio applications.
- Synchronous belts hold tolerances closely even after break in.

DISADVANTAGES OF BELT DRIVES

- Belts are more easily damaged by oil, grease, and heat.
- Belts cannot be used where exact timing or speed is required (unless a special timing belt is used).

Types of Belts

Seven major types of belts are used in modern belt drives:

- **Round belts**
- **Flat belts**
- **V-belts**
- **Banded V-belts**
- **V-ribbed belts**
- **Linked V-belts**
- **Timing belts**
- **Serpentine belts**

Let's look at each belt in detail.

ROUND BELTS

JDPX 1522

Fig. 1 — Round Belt

Round belts (Fig. 1) are usually made of solid rubber or rubber with cords. These belts are normally made for relatively light loads, such as sewing machines and movie projectors. However, larger round belts are sometimes used on farm equipment.

FLAT BELTS

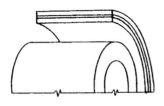

JDPX 1523

Fig. 2 — Flat Belts

Use of flat belts (Fig. 2) has decreased because most machines today have built-in drives or use V-belts. Their most common use is in drives where high power is needed for a separate machine. Examples: old-time threshers and sawmills.

JDPX 1524

Fig. 3 — Flat Belts Are Used on a Round Baler

Flat belts are also used as conveyor belts where the belt itself performs the work, such as on conveyors, draper belts and round baler belts (Fig. 3).

Disadvantages of flat belts are that they need larger pulleys and so take more space; they are also less flexible than some other belts.

Advantages are simplicity, strength, low first cost, and resistance to extreme dust.

On continuous drives, automatic tension on the flat belt is needed. To maintain tension, the drive pulley is often mounted on a motor with a slide rail or pivoted base. Idler pulleys are usually avoided because they put a reverse bend on the belt.

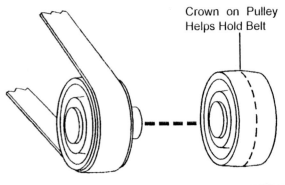

Crown on Pulley
Helps Hold Belt

JDPX 1525

Fig. 4 — Crown Helps Keep Flat Belt on Pulley

Pulleys for flat belts are most often cast iron, steel or wood, and usually are crowned at the center to help keep the belt on the pulley (Fig. 4).

Flat belts are usually made of leather, rubberized fabric and cord. Both rubber and leather in a variety of designs are available for operation in adverse conditions—oil, heat, static electricity and moisture. All these conditions reduce friction, cause the belt to slip and wear excessively.

Leather belts are normally made of tanned steer hides. The belts are formed into single, double, or multiple layers and may be combined with other materials such as cords, fabric, and polymers. Leather belts are also made in links for heavy slow-speed drives with possible high slippage.

Flat rubber belts are made from fabric or cord impregnated with natural or synthetic rubber compounds. These give varying degrees of strength, stretch, pulley grip, and protection against abrasion, oil and moisture.

Flat fabric belts are made from 3 to 12 plies, depending on width. The fabric can be cotton or synthetic fiber with or without rubber impregnation. Load and speed characteristics are moderate. Such belts are usually supplied endless; straight lengths can also be spliced in the field.

Flat cord belts are made from cotton or synthetic material, and are usually supplied endless. They are generally heavy-duty belts used for high-speed, small-pulley and shock-load applications. Steel-cable belts can serve similarly; they have higher capacity and lower stretch than cord constructions.

Perfect alignment of pulleys and belt is a must for good operation of flat belts.

Tension should be no more than needed to transmit the load with the least slippage. However, tension is normally greater than that for V-belts.

V-BELTS

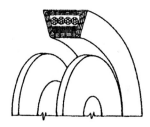

JDPX 1526

Fig. 5 — V-Belt

NOTE: "Pulleys" used with V-belt drives are often called "sheaves." Either term is correct.

V-belts are the most common way of driving loads between short-range pulleys or sheaves (Fig. 5). The simple wedging action of the belt against the sides of the sheave groove is the outstanding feature of V-belts. A greater pull or load merely results in a tighter belt grip.

JDPX 1527

Fig. 6 — V-Belt Drive Using Multiple Belts

Multiple belts are used to meet the power requirements of the application (Fig. 6).

Advantages of V-belts are:

* Wedging action permits lower arc of contact on small pulley and a large speed ratio.

* Shorter center distances can be used for a compact drive and use of streamlined belt guards.

* Absorb shocks to cushion motors and bearings against load fluctuations.

* Vibration and noise levels are low.

* Maintenance and replacements are quick and easy.

* Power transmission efficiency is as high as 94% to 98% after break in.

V-belts are limited, with exceptions, to a practical speed range of 1000 to 10,000 feet per minute (200 to 3000 meters per minute). Some manufacturers recommend 4500 fpm (1375 meters per minute) as the most efficient speed.

Special drives can be designed for 10,000 fpm (3000 meters per minute) or more, but sheaves here require dynamic balancing to reduce the effect of centrifugal force.

Another limitation is the need to match belts in multiple drives to assure equal distribution of load among all the belts. (Banded V-belts are one solution to this problem.)

V-Belt Construction

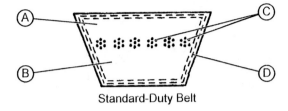
Standard-Duty Belt

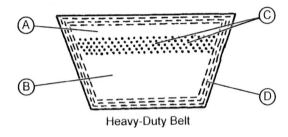
Heavy-Duty Belt

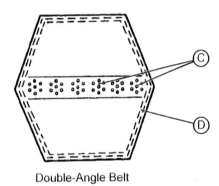
Double-Angle Belt

JDPX 1528

Fig. 7 — Construction Of Common V-Belts

V-belts are made in several types (Fig. 7), but each one is made up of four sections.

The top section of the belt is known as the tension section (Fig 7, A). It is rubber and stretches as the belt forms around the sheave.

The bottom section is called the compression section (Fig 7, B) because it compresses when wedged into and shaped around the sheave.

The center section of the belt is known as the strength section (Fig 7, C). It neither compresses nor stretches, but the cords located in this area give the belt its tensile strength. Without these cords, a V-belt would be pulled in two.

Wrapped or covered belts have a cover section of tough fabric and rubber (Fig 7, D), which protects the inner parts. Covered belts are designed for general applications that require smooth starts, where heavy shock loads are encountered, and backside idler drives may be used.

Heavy-duty belts use a different material for the cords and may use a heavier fabric cover than standard-duty belts.

Double-angle V-belts are used for serpentine drive applications where both the top and bottom of the belt must transmit power to the sheaves. In these belts, the strength cords are in the center of the belt and both the top and bottom of the belt will absorb compression and tension forces. Double-angle V-belts flex equally well in both directions. Both sides of the belt: provide natural wedging action and transmit maximum power regardless of which side of the belt engages the sheave.

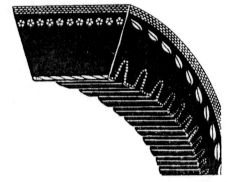

JDPX 1529

Fig. 8 — Corrugated (Notched) V-Belt

Some V-belts do not have a fabric cover. They have straight, "raw edge" or "cut edge" sidewalls (Fig. 8). These belts provide an anti-slip friction surface, greater flexibility, and usually have higher horsepower (kW) ratings than covered belts.

Some V-belts also have a corrugated underside for greater flexibility (Fig. 8). Due to their flexibility, these belts provide longer life and more efficient operation than ordinary wedge-type V-belts.

JDPX 1530

Fig. 9 — Connector-Type V-Belt

Most V-belts are endless, but open-end types are produced for use where a closed belt cannot be installed, or for an emergency replacement of an endless V-belt. The belt ends have metal fasteners joined by a pin, or a link and two pins (Fig. 9).

For more on V-belt design, see page 9, "Operation of V-Belt Drives".

BANDED V-BELTS

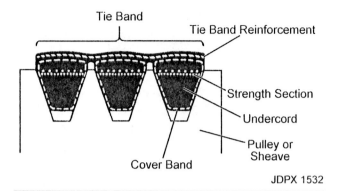

Fig. 10 — Construction of Banded V-Belt

Banded V-belts are multiple belts which have been permanently vulcanized to a tie band (Fig. 10). These belts are designed to reduce problems on multiple-belt drives that are subjected to pulsating loads of extreme vibration where single belts may whip, turn over, or jump off the sheaves.

Banded V-belts are available in the conventional wedge-type V-belt design and in the corrugated or notched-type V-belt design.

Banded V-belts must ride slightly higher in the sheave grooves to provide clearance between the tie band and the sheave flange, otherwise, belt slippage may occur if the tie band contacts the sheave flange. Because of this, sheave groove wear is more critical for banded V-belts than for multiple strands of belts. Also, because the belts are banded together, alignment of the sheaves is somewhat more critical than for multiple strands of V-belts. The same belt tension can be used for banded V-belts as for multiple strands of V-belts.

V-RIBBED BELTS

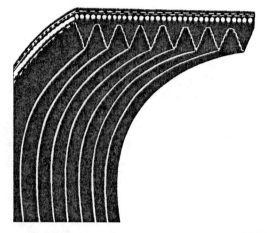

JDPX 1536

Fig. 11 — V-Ribbed Belt

V-ribbed belts (Fig. 11) are an outgrowth of the ordinary V-belt. It combines the strength and simplicity of the flat belt with the positive tracking of V-belts. V-ribbed belts eliminate the matching problem in multi-V-belts, although the sheaves must be grooved to mate precisely with the belt. The sheaves must also be precisely aligned.

V-ribbed belts are made of molded rubber. A ply of strength cords run across the "flat" section of the belt. Most of these are oil- and heat-resistant and will conduct static electricity.

Unlike V-belts, which depend on wedging action to transmit power, V-ribbed belts depend entirely on friction between the sheave and belt. Tension is somewhat greater than for conventional V-belts.

Recommended speeds for V-ribbed belts are in the range of 200 to 10,000 fpm (60 to 3000 meters per minute) for up to 10-hp (7.5 kW) ratings. Most of the effective applications are on small sheaves and short centers.

LINKED V-BELTS

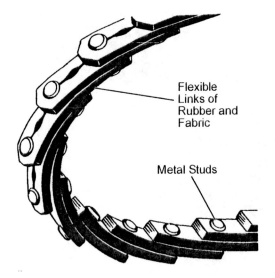

Fig. 12 — Linked V-Belt

Link-type V-belts (Fig. 12) simplify assembly of multiple-belt drives where it would be difficult to match the length of each belt, especially on large fixed-center drives. Links can be added or removed to match the drive.

Link-type belting is also used as an emergency replacement when a standard V-belt is not readily available or for drives where an endless V-belt cannot be installed.

This belt has most of the advantages of the V-belt, except that it is not recommended for speeds over 5000 feet per minute (1525 meters per minute) and can only transmit light loads.

A minor disadvantage: The individual links add up to a larger area exposed to weathering and moisture. This requires extra rubber-sealing protection.

The flexible links are laminated of tough fabric and rubber and are held by metal studs secured with washers. The links are shaped so that the sides of the complete belt fit a standard sheave groove.

SYNCHRONOUS (TIMING) BELTS

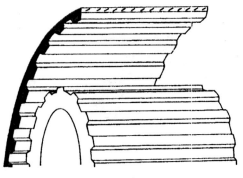

JDPX 1538

Fig. 13 — Timing Belt

Timing belts (Fig. 13) combine chain and sprocket action with the simplicity of flat belts. They are characterized by little slippage and speed variation in ALL models and designs.

They are essentially flat belts with teeth, equally spaced on the surface, in contact with a "toothed pulley" or sprocket.

Continuous, helical wound tensile cords are embedded in the belt as the load-carrying element. The tensile cords are commonly made from steel cables, fiberglass, polyester, or an aramid fiber such as Kevlar. Polyurethane backing and teeth are bonded to the tensile cords to provide shear resistance and protection from dust, oil, and moisture.

Like gear and chain drives, these drives require precise alignment of pulleys and must be made endless.

Advantages of timing belts:

- They require no lubrication.

- No slippage or speed variation.

- The teeth are rigid yet flexible lengthwise, reducing stretch.

- Little maintenance is required.

- Wide range of load and speed, from fractional horsepower to 60 hp (45 kW).

- Lowest bearing loads of any belt drive, because of positive tooth action.

- Compact because of small pulleys, short centers, narrow belts and high capacity.

- Good mechanical efficiency because of no friction, reduced initial tension, and thin construction.

- High horsepower-to-weight ratio.

Other synchronous belts include teeth design and pitch variations to handle many situations that require timing and accurate and efficient power delivery. They are used for power transmission, positioning, and other jobs requiring precision interfacing between the drive and driven shaft.

SERPENTINE BELTS

The serpentine belt design is one that drives several components from a single drive source. Most often used in tractors and other vehicles, the serpentine design can operate AC compressors, water pumps, power steering and more (Fig. 14). It is a simple, mechanically efficient, space-saving and reliable design.

The most obvious disadvantage of the serpentine design as compared to multiple belt systems is that if it fails, all the systems that depend on the belt also fail. The greatest advantage of the serpentine design is that it offers an efficient and reliable way to drive several systems in a limited space. This is done with a single serpentine belt.

A central feature of the serpentine design is the automatic tensioner. This device eliminates the need for tensioning adjustments or special idlers. As loads increase and decrease, the tensioner automatically adjusts the belt tension appropriately. This automatic adjusting takes place through the entire range of normal rpm conditions.

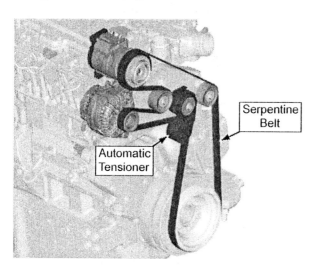

TX1100018

Fig. 14 — Serpentine Belt Application

COMPARISON OF BELTS

This chart compares the qualities of six major belt types.

COMPARISON OF SIX BELT TYPES						
	Flat Belt	**Ordinary V-Belt**	**Linked V-Belt V-Belt**	**Timing Belt**	**V-Ribbed V-Belt**	**Serpentine Belt**
Tension-Bearing Loads	Highest	Low	Low	Lowest	High	High
Best Operating Range, fpm (meters per minute)	1,000 to 10,000 (300 to 3000)	1,000 to 10,000 (300 to 3000)	1,000 to 5,000 (300 to 1525)	1,000 to 10,000 (300 to 3000)	1,000 to 6,000 (300 to 1830)	1,000 to 10,000 (300 to 3000)
Performance above 5000 fpm (1525 meters per minute)	Good	Fair	Not recommended	Good	Fair	Good
Performance below 1000 fpm (300 meters per minute)	Fair	Fair	Fair	Good	Fair	Good
Resistance to shock loads	Good	Good	Good	Fair	Good	Fair
Mechanical Efficiency	Good	Good	Good	Best	Good	Good
Ease of Belt Splice	Good in some types	Good in some types	Excellent	(Endless belt)	(Endless belt)	(Endless belt)
Misalignment Tolerance	None	Compensates best	Compensates best	None	None	Compensates best
Minimum downtime	Good	Best	Best	Good	Good	Good
Noisiness	Most	Very little	Little	Little	Little	Very little
Synchronous operations	No	No	No	Yes	No	No
Creep	Some	Negligible	Some	None	Some	Some
Initial Cost	Low	Low	Moderate	High	Moderate	High
Resistance to weather	Good	Good	Fair	Good	Good	Good
Maintenance needed	Some	Negligible	Some	Negligible	Some	Some

Operation of V-Belt Drives

Because they are so common, let's look at the operation of V-belt drives in more detail.

HOW A V-BELT GRIPS

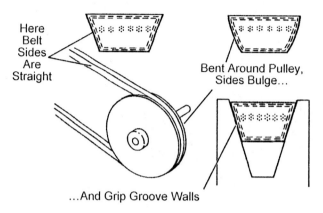

Here Belt Sides Are Straight

Bent Around Pulley, Sides Bulge...

...And Grip Groove Walls

JDPX 1539

Fig. 15 — How a V-Belt Grips

Due to the wedging action of their angled sides, V-belts pull well. The section going around a pulley tends to bulge as it bends, hugging the flanges tightly (Fig. 15).

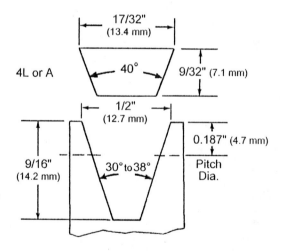

4L or A

17/32" (13.4 mm)

40°

9/32" (7.1 mm)

1/2" (12.7 mm)

9/16" (14.2 mm)

30° to 38°

0.187" (4.7 mm)

Pitch Dia.

JDPX 1540

Fig. 16 — Belt and Sheave Groove Dimensions

The angle between the standard belt sides is 40 degrees; the angle between the two sides of the pulley (or sheave) groove is somewhat less to ensure full wedging contact (Fig. 16).

The groove is much deeper than the belt, because a standard V-belt must never ride the bottom of the groove. If if does, it loses almost all traction, no matter how taut.

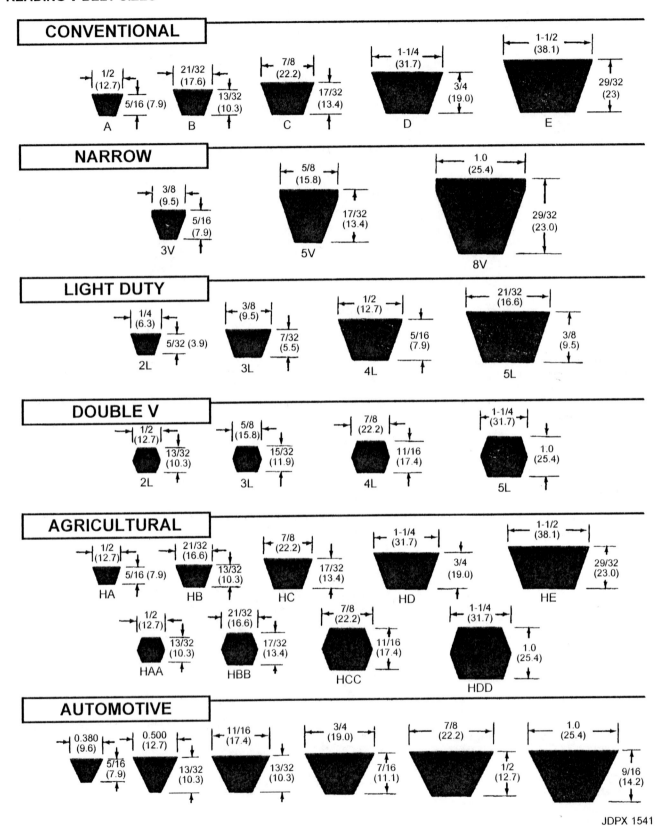

Fig. 17 — Types and Sizes of V-Belts (Numbers in Parentheses Indicate Size in Millimeters)

JDPX 1541

V-belts are made in the various types and sizes (Fig. 17). Industry codes are shown below each belt cross section and widths and depths for each size are included.

The widths of common V-belts range from 1/4 in. (6.3 mm) to 1 1/2 in. (38.1 mm), but you will rarely find these fractions on a belt. Markings usually show the width, duty type, and length of the belt in a simple code, but the code varies among manufacturers.

In a typical belt marking such as 4L410, for example, the 4 stands for 1/2 in. nominal width, the "L" for light duty, and the next three digits for the belt length in inches—the last digit indicates tenths of an inch (usually zero, meaning no fraction; or 5, for 1/2 in. The 4L410 belt is therefore 41.0 inches long.

Some belts have a metric code or part number, based on an industry standard system, in addition to the manufacturer's English coding system. The metric equivalent of the English belt marking 4L410, discussed in the example above, is 13R1040. The first digit or digits stand for the nominal belt width in millimeters, 13 mm in this example. The duty type marking "R" is for light duty and is the equivalent of the English marking "L." The last digits stand for the belt length in millimeters, 1040 mm in this example.

NOTE: Although belt manufacturers use similar belt numbering systems, different brands with the same number will differ slightly in dimensions. Also, construction differences cause them to ride differently in the sheave grooves, and to stretch differently. Therefore, belts from different manufacturers cannot be matched together and should not be mixed on multiple-belt drives.

Each type of belt comes in a wide range of lengths.

When replacing a belt, try to use the figures on the old belt. If they're not legible, don't measure the belt—it will have stretched. Pull a steel tape around the outside of the two pulleys, first slacking off the tensioning adjustment to one quarter of its take-up distance. You'll need the remaining three-quarters to take up the initial stretch of a new belt, and a little more from time to time, for V-belts get longer—never shorter—in use.

Never buy a belt so tight that it has to be pried over the sheaves. This breaks the pulling cords inside. Always buy the belt to suit the job.

PULLEYS OR SHEAVES

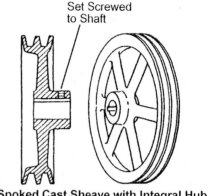

Set Screwed to Shaft

Spoked Cast Sheave with Integral Hub

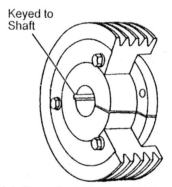

Keyed to Shaft

Disk-Type Cast Sheave with Removable Hub

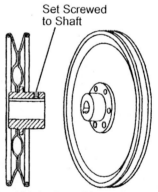

Set Screwed to Shaft

Formed Steel Light-Duty Sheave with Integral Hub

JDPX 1542

Fig. 18 — Types Of Sheaves For V-Belt Drives

For most V-belt drives, sheaves are available in formed steel or cast iron. Typical sheaves are shown in Fig. 18.

Standard sheaves are made with either regular or deep grooves. A deep-groove sheave is generally used whenever the V-belt enters the sheave at an angle—as, for example, in a quarter-turn drive—on vertical shaft drives, or wherever belt stability is a problem.

Applications

Formed-steel sheaves are used primarily in light-duty applications (2L, 3L, 4L, and 5L belts), and in automotive or agricultural service.

Cast-iron sheaves are used in all types of V-belt drives. They are almost always used in applications with fluctuating loads, where flywheel effect is important.

Special Sheaves

Sheaves can be made of a number of materials other than formed steel and cast iron. V-belt sheaves are sometimes steel or aluminum alloy. For some very light-duty applications, plastic or die-cast sheaves are used.

Where operating conditions are severe, special materials such as stainless steel are sometimes used.

Frequently, a less expensive solution is to use a cast-iron sheave coated with a special finish, such as a black oxide. These sheaves are especially resistant to abrasion.

Hubs

Formed-steel sheaves almost always have an integral hub. Multiple-V and ribbed-V sheaves are made with either integral or interchangeable bushings to fit various shaft sizes.

Most sheaves are keyed to their shafts and then either set-screwed or secured with a hex nut and lock washer.

Numbers of Grooves

Multiple-V sheaves are generally stocked in the following numbers of grooves: A and B sections, 1 to 10 grooves; C, 1 to 12; D, 3 to 20.

Balancing of Sheaves

Most standard sheaves are statically balanced and are satisfactory for rim speeds up to 6000 fpm (1830 meters per minute). Most narrow-belt sheaves are satisfactory for rim speeds up to 6500 fpm (1980 meters per minute). In some cases a special design or special materials may also be needed.

How Pulley Sizes Affect Power Output

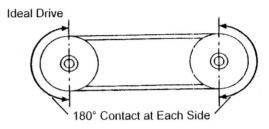

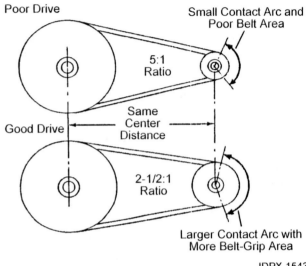

Fig. 19 — How Pulley Sizes Affect Power Output

For full power on the belt, the pulley ratio should be 3 to 1 or less (Fig. 19). Higher ratios (shown) lessen the arc of contact, causing slippage and loss of power.

When sheaves are too small for the belt cross section, the belt flexes beyond its normal limits. This can result in cracks on the underside of the belt. In most cases, the use of a belt with a cogged or corrugated underside in place of the conventional V-belt will improve the belt service life greatly, due to the greater flexibility of the cogged belt.

Another problem resulting from the use of sheaves that are too small is that insufficient belt wrap on the smaller sheave can require excessive belt tension to prevent slippage. This can cause overheating of the motor bearings, or even bent shafts.

The arc of contact on the critical smaller pulley increases somewhat if the shafts are moved farther apart. Where a high ratio is required, it is best to use a two-step drive (that is, a countershaft) to avoid the use of excessive single-step ratios or an undersize pulley.

RELATIVE OUTPUT SPEED OF BELT DRIVES

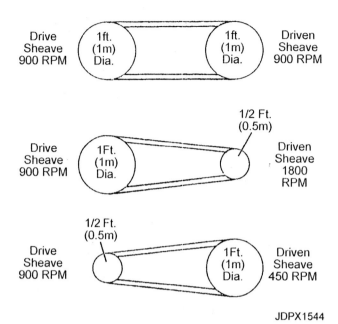

JDPX1544

Fig. 20 — Relative Output Speed of Belt Drives

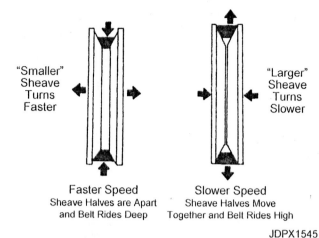

JDPX1545

Fig. 21 — Variable-Speed Belt Drive

When the **drive** and **driven** pulleys or sheaves are of the same size (Fig. 20, top), they will rotate at the same speed (rpm).

If we keep the same **drive** sheave but use a smaller **driven** sheave (Fig. 20, center), the driven shaft will turn *faster.*

If we use a smaller **drive** sheave but keep the **driven** sheave the same (Fig. 20, bottom), the driven shaft will turn *slower.*

The formula for this is:

Diameter Drive Sheave	x	RPM of Drive Sheave	=	Diameter Driven Sheave	x	RPM of Driven Sheave

In Fig. 20 we can see how this works (top to bottom):

$$1 \times 900 = 1 \times \mathbf{900}$$
$$1 \times 900 = 1/2 \times \mathbf{1800}$$
$$1/2 \times 900 = 1 \times \mathbf{450}$$

VARIABLE-SPEED BELT DRIVES

Variable speed is obtained by changing the effective diameter of the sheave or sheaves during operation.

The variable-speed sheave is made up of two movable halves. By moving the halves together, the driven sheave becomes "larger" since the belt now rides higher in the sheave "V" (Fig. 21) and the sheave turns at a slower speed.

When the sheave halves are moved apart, the driven sheave becomes "smaller" (Fig. 21) and the sheave turns at a faster rate.

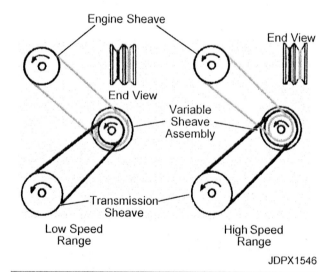

JDPX1546

Fig. 22 — Variable-Diameter Sheave Operation

Some variable-speed belt drives use a dual pulley variable-diameter sheave assembly (Fig. 22). A belt from the fixed-diameter sheave on the power source drives one side of the variable-diameter sheave assembly. Another belt on the other side of the variable-diameter sheave assembly drives the fixed-diameter sheave on the input shaft of the powered equipment.

A typical aplication for variable-speed control might be a congeyor system as shown in Fig. 23. In this type of system, a varible-speed sheave and motor drives a fixed pulley sometimes called a companion pulley. With the motor operating at a constant speed, the conveyor speed is adjusted by changing the adjustable sheaves attached to the motor.

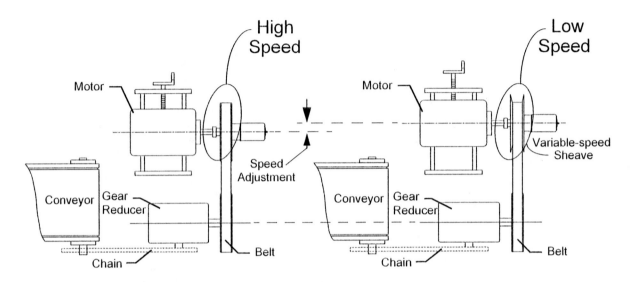

JDPX8170

Fig. 23 — Variable-speed Sheave Application

A **low speed range** is provided when the variable-speed driven pulley becomes "larger" and the variable-speed drive pulley becomes "smaller." A **high speed range** is provided when the variable-speed driven pulley becomes "smaller" and the variable-speed drive pulley becomes "larger."

When the sheave sizes are changed, the belt tension also changes. So there must be a means of "taking up the slack." This may be done in any of these ways:

- Moving the sheaves closer together when the sheave diameter becomes "larger," or farther apart when the sheave diameter becomes "smaller." (A spring-loaded sheave can do this.)

- Using an idler on the belt which responds to tension or slackening.

- Using two variable-pitch sheaves. The sheaves are synchronized so that when one changes its size, the other changes to offset it.

Variable speed drives can be manually or automatically controlled.

ARRANGEMENT OF V-BELT DRIVES

Most common is the **reduction drive**, in which the power source turns faster than the driven shaft.

Less common are these:

- **Speed-up drive**, where the load must run faster than the motor or engine, is considered harder on belts.

- **V-flat drive** is a reduction drive with a V-pulley on the motor and a flat one on the driven shaft. It's used in industry and on some lathe countershafts. To be effective, a V-flat drive should have a big ratio and short shaft spacing, to allow plenty of wraparound on the sheave. The sheave should have a perfectly flat face—not a crowned one.

RIGGING QUARTER-TURN AND ANGLED DRIVES

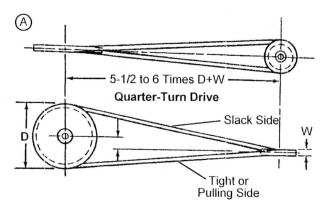

Quarter-Turn Drive

5-1/2 to 6 Times D+W

Slack Side

Tight or Pulling Side

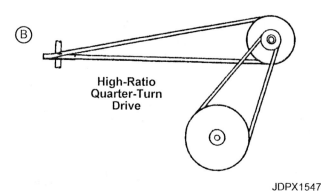

High-Ratio Quarter-Turn Drive

JDPX1547

Fig. 24 — Quarter-Turn V-Belt Drives

Critical alignment is the mark of a successful quarter-turn drive (Fig. 24, A). Expect them to carry only 75 percent as much power as equivalent normal drives. Ignore dimensions W for single-belt use, but figure offset 1/4 to keep the taut side of the belt as parallel to the small sheave as possible. If greater than 2-1/2:1 ratio is needed, use the two-step drive (Fig. 24, B). With idler-angle drives (Fig. 25) spacing must allow a 90-degree twist at each side of idlers, but the angles of the two shafts may vary widely around idler centers.

- **Quarter-turn drives** twist the belt through 90 degrees. Deep-groove pulleys are used, and the shafts are offset to bring them taut, or pull the side of the belt more parallel to the groove at the smaller sheave. The belt is mounted so that the tight side is at the bottom—minimizing the sag that tends to pull it off the sheaves. This drive gives only about 75 percent of the power capacity of a normal drive with the same belt-speed-sheave combination.

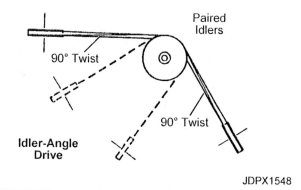

Paired Idlers

90° Twist

90° Twist

Idler-Angle Drive

JDPX1548

Fig. 25 — Angled V-Belt Drives

- **Idler-angle drives** between horizontal and vertical, or otherwise angled shafts, subject the belt to two 90-degree twists (Fig. 25). Distances from the idlers to both shafts must be generous. Deep-groove idlers are used to prevent the belt from riding itself ragged on shallow groove edges.

- **Dual and multi-drives.** Using two 3L belts can transmit more power than a single 5L belt where shaft spacing and pulley sizes are limited. Industrial machines may have multi-grooved pulleys with several ganged V-belts. Belts pulling together should be matched—of the same make and length, or bought as a matched set—and replaced as a group, never singly.

BELT TENSION MECHANISMS

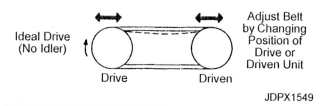

Ideal Drive (No Idler)

Adjust Belt by Changing Position of Drive or Driven Unit

Drive   Driven

JDPX1549

Fig. 26 — Ideal Drive with No Idler

In many successful belt drives, an idler is not necessary, and proper tension can be had by adjusting the position of either the drive unit or the driven unit (Fig. 26). (An exception is the variable-load drive, where a spring-loaded idler is still best for longer belt life.)

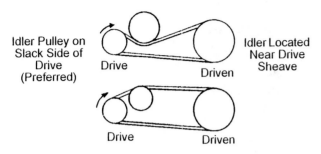

Idler Pulley on Slack Side of Drive (Preferred)

Drive

Driven

Idler Located Near Drive Sheave

Drive

Driven

JDPX1550

Fig. 27 — Idler Pulley Located on Slack Side (Preferred)

Where the sheaves are not adjustable, a belt tightener with an **idler** pulley or sheave is used (Fig. 27). The idler may be a straight-face pulley running on the outside of the belts, or a grooved sheave or a straight-face pulley running on the inside of the belts. The arcs of contact on the driving and driven sheaves are increased by an idler on the outside and decreased by an idler on the inside.

The idler should preferably run on the **slack** side of the belts. A straight-face idler pulley running on either the outside or inside of the belts should be located as close as possible to the sheave delivering (not receiving) the belts (Fig. 27). Hence, an idler pulley running on the slack side of belts should be close to the drive sheave.

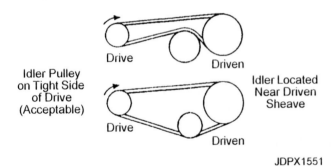

Drive

Driven

Idler Pulley on Tight Side of Drive (Acceptable)

Drive

Idler Located Near Driven Sheave

Driven

JDPX1551

Fig. 28 — Idler Pulley Located on Tight Strand (Acceptable)

If an idler pulley must run on the **tight** side, it should be close to the driven sheave (Fig. 28). A grooved idler sheave running on the inside of the belts may be near either sheave but preferably is located to give equal arcs of contact on both sheaves.

Idler diameter should be at least one-third larger than the smallest sheave in the drive when running on the outside of the belts—at least as large as the smallest sheave when running on the inside of the belts.

A *spring-loaded* or weighted idler pulley is sometimes used. This type of idler should be located on the slack side of the drive. It should not be used on a drive where the slack side may temporarily become the tight side.

Maintenance of V-Belt Drives

Due to the fact that the belts and sheaves wear gradually during normal operation, a periodic inspection of the belt drive will allow you to spot potential problems early and arrange scheduled maintenance of the drive, thereby avoiding an unexpected failure. An unexpected failure of a belt drive is usually a sign that something else in the system is wrong.

Several factors influence how often you need to inspect a belt drive. Drives operating at high speeds, heavy loads, frequent stop/start conditions, and at temperature extremes. Operating on critical equipment will require frequent inspection.

PRACTICE SAFE MAINTENANCE

⚠ **CAUTION: Never attempt to adjust a belt while it is operating. Keep hands, feet, and clothing away.**

A safe working environment must be established when servicing a belt drive. The following precautions will make belt drive inspection and maintenance easier and safer:

- Always shut off the power to the drive and wait for all parts to stop moving before doing any maintenance work on power drives. Lock the controlling switch In the OFF position if possible.

- Make sure that the machine drive components are in a neutral position to avoid accidental movement or startup.

Pinch Points

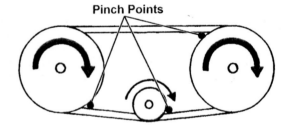

JDPX1552

Fig. 29 — Pinch Points on Rotating Parts Can Catch Clothing, Hands, Arms, and Feet

- Avoid hazardous pinch points (Fig. 29) on the rotating parts of the belt drive. Manufacturers build shields for pinch points. Always replace shields if you must remove them to repair or adjust the belt drive.

- Maintain a safe access to belt drives. Keep the area around the drives clean and free of clutter, debris, and other obstructions.

CAUTION: Never attempt to adjust a belt while it is operating. Keep hands, feet, and clothing away.

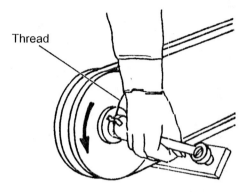

Thread

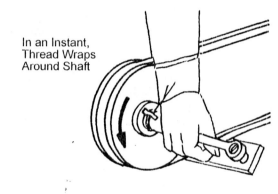

In an Instant, Thread Wraps Around Shaft

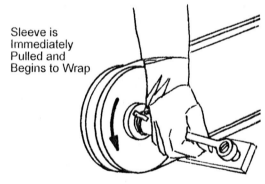

Sleeve is Immediately Pulled and Begins to Wrap

JDPX1553

Fig. 30 — Wrapping May Begin with Just a Thread

- Wear proper clothing when working around rotating components that are a potential wrap point. Never wear loose, bulky or ragged clothes around belt drives. Often, the wrapping begins with just a thread or frayed piece of cloth catching on the rotating part (Fig. 30). More fibers wrap around the shaft as it continues to rotate, pulling you into the drive in a split second.

- Use caution while inspecting sheaves or sprockets to avoid being cut by burrs or sharply worn pulley edges.

MECHANICAL INTERFERENCE

One of the chief advantages of V-belt drives is ease of inspection. By watching and listening, signs of normal wear can be detected.

A belt striking against the belt guard produces an audible "ticking" sound that warns of rubbing contact. This contact can produce rapid wear of the fabric on wrapped belts and will greatly shorten the life of the belt. Where the noise of nearby equipment might drown out the "ticking," routine visual inspection for bent or damaged belt guards will also reveal belt guard contact. Of course, the belt will probably be frayed—another sign of rubbing.

SHEAVE MISALIGNMENT

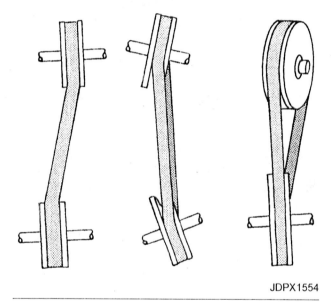

JDPX1554

Fig. 31 — Sheaves Not Aligned Can Damage the V-Belt

Sheave misalignment is another problem to watch for during routine inspection. While the misalignment illustrated in Fig. 31 is exaggerated, it does indicate another common cause of shortened belt life.

Sheave misalignment can cause rapid wear of the V-belt sidewalls and considerably shorten the service life of both the belt and sheaves. Misalignment can also cause belts to turn over or jump off the sheaves. Angular misalignment of the sheaves can also give the appearance that individual belts of a multiple-belt drive are mismatched.

As a general rule, V-belts can tolerate misalignment of up to 1/16 in. (1.6 mm) per 12 in. (305 mm) of shaft center distance. The greater the belt misalignment, the greater the chance of belt instability.

Sheaves are usually out of line because the drive and driven shafts are not parallel. However, even perfectly parallel shafts do not guarantee sheave alignment.

Fig. 31 shows three basic types of sheave misalignment. In the example shown on the left, the shafts are parallel, but the sheaves are not in line. The drive or driven sheave must be moved in or out on its shaft for proper alignment.

NOTE: The sheave should be mounted as close to the shaft bearing as possible to reduce overhung load on the bearing.

The other two examples of sheave misalignment (center, right) are the result of angular misalignment. To correct the misalignment, the drive and driven shafts must be repositioned so the shafts are parallel and the sheaves are aligned.

JDPX1556

Fig. 33 — Mismatched Belts

Fig. 33 shows mismatched belts. This drive has seven new belts, but one (arrow) is getting a "free ride." Although all belts are new, the outside belt is obviously longer and not pulling its share of the load.

When watching for possible mismatching, look for sagging belts on the tight side of the drive—the side on which the belts approach the motor. If they are even on this side (even though not too even on the slack side), the belts are pulling their fair share of the load.

To ensure proper belt matching, V-belts are marked with belt size numbers.

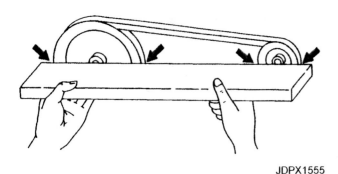

JDPX1555

Fig. 32 — Check Alignment of Sheaves

Possibly the best way to check alignment is to use a straight edge between the sides of the sheaves (Fig. 32).

The straight edge should touch the sheaves at the four arrows. Then rotate each sheave and note whether the contact of either sheave with the straight edge is disturbed. If so, a shaft is bent or a sheave is wobbling.

Another method is to sight across the edge of the sheave groove in line with the belt. Harmful misalignment will show up as a bend in the belt at the point where it enters or leaves the sheave grooves.

V-belts, because of their flexibility, can tolerate more misalignment than other types of power drives. But there is a point beyond which they should not be misaligned if they are to deliver the service they are designed to give.

MISMATCHED BELTS

In multiple-belt drives, the belts must be accurately matched so that the load is evenly distributed among the belts. If the load isn't evenly distributed, the shorter belts will do all the work.

WORN BELTS

JDPX1557

Fig. 34 — Replacing Only One Belt in a Set Means Overloading the New Belt and Underloading the Others

All belts and sheaves wear to some degree after they have been in use. As wear occurs the belts ride lower in the sheave grooves. Since the center distance has to be increased to compensate for the wear, a worn belt is "longer" than a new belt. (The worn belt also stretches in use.)

It is important, therefore, to **replace the entire set on multiple-belt drives** even though only one belt might fail. If only one belt is replaced, the replacement will in effect be "shorter" than the other belts (Fig. 34).

Because the old belts are worn and stretched, the new belt is pulling most of the load. And, since seven belts are obviously needed to meet the horsepower (kW) requirements of the application, the overload will considerably shorten the life of the new belt.

JDPX1558

Fig. 35 — Replace All Belts in a Set at One Time as Shown

In Fig. 35, all belts in the set have been replaced and each belt is carrying an equal share of the load. When belts pull together like this, they'll give the service they're designed to provide.

It isn't expensive to replace all belts on a multiple-belt drive when only one has failed. It's insurance against forced downtime and lost production.

BELT TENSION

Too little tension will cause slippage or slip-and-grab, causing the belt to break. If the belt does not break, slip will cause excessive cover wear, burned spots, and overheating.

Too much tension will cause belt heating and excessive stretch as well as damage to drive components such as sheaves and shafts. The extra tightness will also place a heavier load on the bearings.

As a general rule the **correct tension** is the lowest tension at which the belts will run and not slip during startup or peak loading.

Remember that V-belts should ride on the sides of standard sheaves, not on the bottom of the groove.

Tension on a new belt should be watched *during the first 24 hours of operation*. This is when the initial seating and stretch occurs.

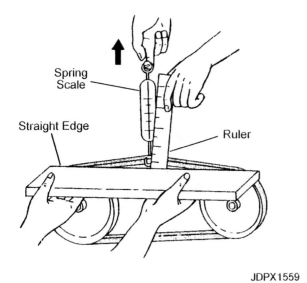

JDPX1559

Fig. 36 — Checking Belt Tension Using a Spring Scale

Belt tension is often checked by deflecting the belt on one side with a spring scale (Fig. 36). By measuring the deflection at a certain pounds pull, actual belt tension is found. The recommended tension is given in the machine operator's manual.

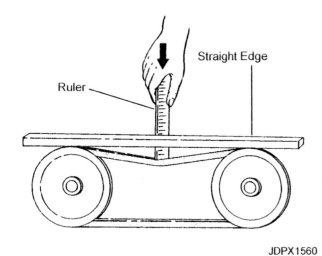

JDPX1560

Fig. 37 — Depressing Belt with Ruler to Check Belt Tension

Another method is to depress the belt halfway between the sheaves using a ruler at right angles to a straight edge (Fig. 37).

Special belt tension tester tools are available from belt distributors and other specialized sources. The tension tester tools measure the force required to deflect the belt a certain distance in a manner similar to that shown in Fig. 38. Instructions for the use of the tension tester will be included with the tool. The belt or equipment manufacturers also provide belt tension specifications for use with the belt tension testers.

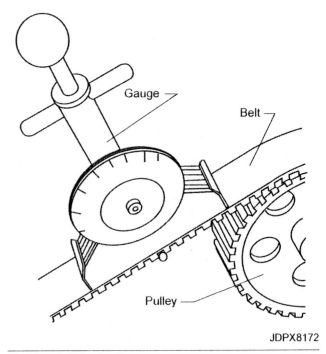

JDPX8172

Fig. 38 — Belt Tension Gauge

Tension on Banded V-Belts

On banded V-belts, the only special consideration is that the entire belt must be deflected uniformly. This can be done by placing a rigid bar, which will extend across the width of the belt, between the tension tester and the belt.

Tension on Quarter-Turn Drives

On these drives, adjust tension so that when the drive is running, the middle belt on the slack side of the drive will not sag below its groove in the sheave on the vertical shaft.

 CAUTION: Never attempt to adjust a belt while it is operating. Keep hands, feet, and clothing away.

BELT SLIP

While loose belts usually cause slippage, the cause may be overload. If belt tension is okay but the belt still slips, overload is the likely problem.

Never attempt to correct slip by using a belt dressing. While reducing slip, the dressing may soften and deteriorate the V-belt.

BELT SQUEAK

Squeak often occurs at idling speeds. It produces a sound very much like the chirping of a bird or a dry bearing and is most prevalent when pressed-steel pulleys are used. Squeak is not unique to certain makes or types of belts. But it is most likely to occur on cold, damp mornings or under dusty conditions.

Squeak itself is harmless, but is frequently mistaken for belt slippage. Consequently, belts are often tightened to a point where they or the bearings are damaged.

Never apply belt dressing or oil as a means of eliminating this noise.

BELT SQUEAL

Squeal is a high-pitched howl or rasping sound that occurs during acceleration or when the belt is near or at overload. It definitely means the belt is slipping and should be investigated. The cause is usually a lack of belt tension.

If the squeal persists after the belts have been checked and tensioned, the drive itself should be checked for overloading. Again, never use belt dressing as a substitute for retensioning the belt.

SHEAVE GROOVE WEAR

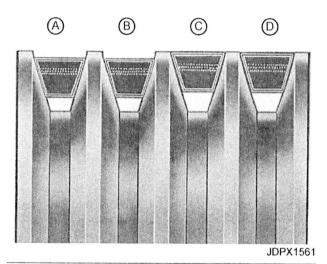

Fig. 39 — Irregular Sheave Grooves

In the four-groove sheave shown in Fig. 39, grooves (A) and (B) are worn much more than the others. This wear allows the belts in the worn grooves to ride lower than the rest of the belts and creates the same effect as mismatched belts.

Also, it causes what is termed "differential driving"—a condition where the belts operate at different speed ratios between the drive and driven units. In such a drive, the belts actually "fight" each other because some of them are trying to travel faster than others.

When mismatched belts are spotted in a multiple-belt drive, the sheave grooves should be examined for excessive wear. On banded V-belts, if the tie band is separating from the belts, this may also mean worn sheave grooves.

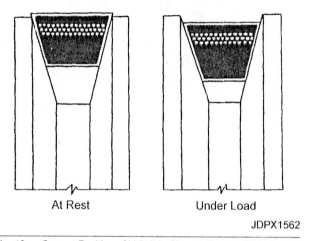

At Rest   Under Load

JDPX1562

Fig. 40 — Correct Position of V-Belt in Sheave Groove (R.M.A. Standard Sheave)

Because of slight variation in V-belts and sheave grooves, the riding position of new belts in new sheaves will vary. In a standard sheave, it will vary from 1/16 in. (1.6 mm) above the top of the grooves to 1/16 in. (1.6 mm) below the top (Fig. 40). However, for a given multiple-groove sheave, the riding positions of the belts should be uniform.

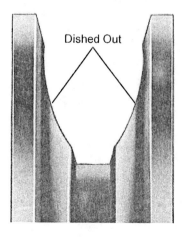

Fig. 41 — Sheave Grooves "Dished Out" by Wear (Replace Sheaves)

A new belt that rides lower than other belts in a drive may mean that the sheave groove sidewall is "dished out" (Fig. 41).

When the groove walls are dished out, the belt's wedging action is reduced. The gripping power is reduced and—in extreme cases—slippage occurs and belt life is greatly shortened.

The wedging principle of V-belt drives makes it vital to keep the sheave groove sidewalls perfectly straight.

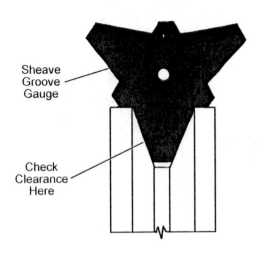

Fig. 42 — Checking Sheave Groove for Wear

Sheave groove wear gauges, which are available from your belt distributor, can be used to check the grooves accurately for wear. Place the correct size wear gauge in the sheave groove and check for clearance between the sides of the gauge and the sidewalls of the sheave (Fig. 42). A bright light, such as a flashlight, held behind the gauge will help you observe the amount of wear. Sheave groove "dishing" should not exceed 1/32 inch (0.8 mm) for individual V-belts, or 1/64 inch (0.4 mm) for banded V-belts.

SHINY SHEAVE GROOVE BOTTOMS

In standard sheaves, a shiny groove bottom is a sign that the belt, or sheave, or both are badly worn and the belt is bottoming in the groove. This causes the belt to lose its grip and waste power.

Worn sheaves or shiny sheave groove bottoms will usually show up first on the smaller sheave of the installation.

WOBBLING SHEAVES

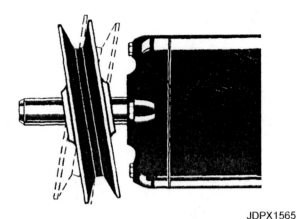

Fig. 43 — Wobbling Sheaves

Wobbling sheaves are another cause of shortened belt life. A wobbling sheave (Fig. 43) whips the belt from side to side, subjecting it to a lateral strain which produces rapid sheave and belt wear. A wobbling sheave also transmits vibrations to the machine.

Sheave wobble is caused by improper installation of the sheave on the shaft, a worn or damaged bushing or sheave hub, improper assembly of split-type bushing and sheave, or by a bent shaft. Sheaves must be installed so that they run true on the shaft to ensure maximum belt life.

A sheave that wobbles badly enough to require adjustment can be readily spotted by visual inspection.

DAMAGED SHEAVES

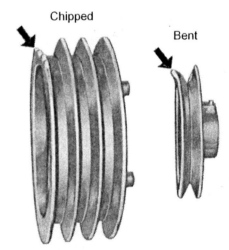

Fig. 44 — Damaged Sheaves

Sometimes sheaves are damaged as shown in Fig. 44. Cast sheaves may become chipped; pressed steel sheaves can get bent.

Regardless of the type of damage to the sheave, damaged sheaves always produce rapid belt wear. The only way to prevent short belt life is to replace the sheave.

REPLACING SHEAVES

If a sheave is excessively worn, bent, cracked, or broken, replace it as follows:

1. Select replacement sheave. Sheave must have the same groove and shaft diameter as the old one. It also must have the same outside diameter. Changing diameters will call for a different length of belt and also will change the speed of the drive.

2. Remove the shields.

3. Loosen tension and carefully remove the belts.

4. Loosen the sheave on the shaft. You may have to loosen a setscrew and remove a key, loosen a sheave flange bolt, remove a split bushing, or remove a retainer nut. On some installations you may have to remove a bearing or two before removing the sheave.

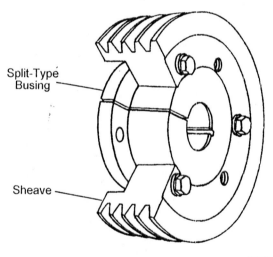

JDPX1567

Fig. 45 — Split-Type Bushing and Sheave

5. On sheaves with split-type bushings (Fig. 45), remove the cap screws attaching the bushing to the sheave. Insert cap screws in the threaded jack-screw holes. Starting with the jack-screw furthest from the bushing split, tighten the jack-screws alternately and progressively until the sheave is separated from the bushing.

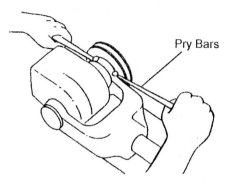

Pry Bars

JDPX1568

Fig. 46 — Removing Sheaves Using Pry Bars

6. For other fasteners, you may be able to pry the sheave off the shaft with a bar. Pry from first one side and then the other (Fig. 46). Do not let the sheave fall freely on a hard surface. Never pound on a sheave with a hammer. Many are metal castings and are easily broken. Do not pry to hard or sheave will be bent.

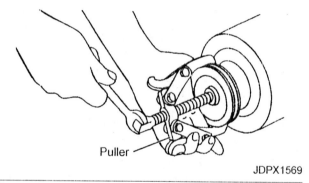

Puller

JDPX1569

Fig. 47 — Removing Sheaves Using Puller

7. If you cannot pry the sheave off easily, use a puller (Fig. 47).

IMPORTANT: A sheave can also be bent or broken with a puller if you are not careful. Tighten the puller, then tap on the end of the puller to jar the sheave loose.

8. Replace with new sheave(s). Sheave should go on by tapping the hub with a plastic or rubber hammer, or drawn into place with the mounting hardware.

IMPORTANT: On sheaves with split-type bushings, make certain that the tapered surface of the bushing and the mating bore of the sheave are free of all foreign substances. Never lubricate the tapered surfaces before assembling. The use of lubricant and/or excessive cap screw torque can cause cracking of the bushing.

9. To install sheaves with split-type bushings (Fig. 45), line up the bolt holes in the bushing with the bolt holes in the sheave. Install the mounting cap screws and tighten evenly to the torque recommended by the manufacturer.

10. Check sheave alignment and correct as necessary. See Page 18.

11. Tighten the sheave on the shaft.

12. Install the belts and adjust tension.

13. Install the shields.

OVERHEATED BELTS

JDPX1570

Fig. 48 — Belt Ruined By Too Much Heat

V-belts are composed mainly of rubber—and heat is the natural enemy of rubber.

When the drive is open or ventilated, the temperature is usually not high enough to affect the belts.

Under field conditions, belts operating in ambient temperatures of less than 140°F (60°C) are not materially affected. Temperatures in excess of 140°F (60°C) may harden the belt causing it to crack and stretch. To prevent this, be sure that screens and shields are kept clean for full ventilation.

The belt internal temperature is the determining factor when heat is a suspected cause of short belt life. For example, a rise in the ambient drive temperature of approximately 36°F (20°C) can result in an internal temperature increase of 18°F (10°C). Tests have shown that an internal temperature increase of 18°F (10°C) may cut the service life of a V-belt in half.

Fig. 48 shows a belt damaged by excessive heat. It appears cracked or checked on the bottom edge and should be replaced.

A general rule for checking the belt for excessive heat without the use of sophisticated instruments is to stop the drive and touch the belt with your hand. Your hand can tolerate up to about 140°F (60°C), the maximum temperature at which a properly maintained belt should operate.

If you can grasp the belt for at least five seconds, the belt temperature is probably not beyond the operating temperature range for most V-belts. However, if the belt is too hot to touch, the belt temperature is probably well over 140°F (60°C), and heat is contributing to short belt life.

Check for belt slippage if the belts get too hot during operation.

Specially compounded heat-resistant belts are available for use where heat is a problem.

OILY OR GREASY BELTS

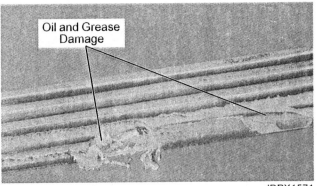

Oil and Grease Damage

JDPX1571

Fig. 49 — Belt Ruined by Oil and Grease Soaking

Oil or grease if allowed to soak into the rubber (Fig. 49) causes a V-belt made of natural rubber—or synthetics—to become soft, to swell, and to deteriorate very rapidly.

 CAUTION: Never try to clean a belt while it is operating.

When oil or grease is found on a belt, first shut off the drive and correct the cause of the oil or grease leakage. The belt and sheave grooves should be cleaned with a clean cloth dampened with a detergent and water mixture. Then wipe the belt dry with a clean dry cloth.

Sanding or scraping the belt with a sharp object to remove grease or oil is not recommended.

For naturally oily or greasy operations, oil-resistant belts can be installed.

INSTALLING V-BELTS

A belt found turned over in the pulley groove should be replaced. Flip-over usually means one or more of the cords in the strength section is broken.

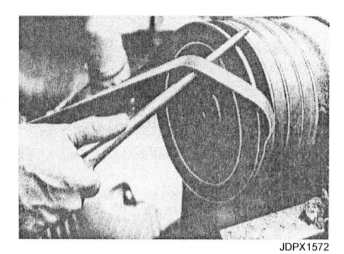

JDPX1572

Fig. 50 — Never Force a V-Belt onto a Sheave

Broken cords can result from prying or forcing belts into sheaves without loosening the idler or drive motor mounting bolts (Fig. 50).

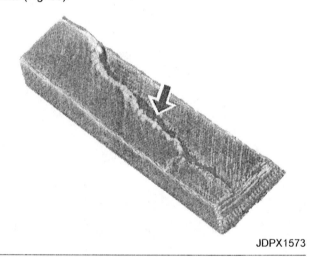

JDPX1573

Fig. 51 — Belt Damaged by Incorrect Installation

A rupture or split in the fabric cover section of wrapped belts (Fig. 51), caused by the prying tool or the sheave edge, is usually an indication of improper belt installation. Broken cords are easily identifiable on raw edge sidewall (non-wrapped) V-belts, because it is usually the edge cords that are damaged first.

The proper method of installing a V-belt is to loosen the idler or drive mounting bolts and position the drive components so that the new belt can be dropped over the sheaves. Now, move the sheaves apart until the belt is seated in the grooves, and check sheave alignment. (See Page 18.) Adjust belt tension. (See Pages 19 and 21.)

Keep all belt guards and shields in place.

Signs of Improper V-Belt Installation

- *Belt stretched beyond take-up*
- *Belt slips*
- *Belt fails rapidly for no visible reason*
- *Belt rolls over*
- *Belt cut on bottom*

STORING V-BELTS

Proper belt storage is important for both new belts and for those on the machine.

Storage In the Shop

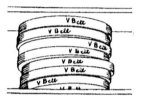

JDPX1574

Fig. 52 — Storing Belts in the Shop

New belts should be stored as follows to keep them factory-fresh:

- Store belts in a clean, cool, dry place. Shrinkage or deterioration may occur if belts are piled on damp floors or stored near radiators.

- Keep belts away from heat and direct sunlight.

- Do not place in bins for long periods which might distort the shape of the belt.

- Do not hang V-belts on small pegs or nails. The pegs should be crescent shaped in cross section to avoid compression dents in the belt from sharp corners. The pegs should also be sufficiently large in cross section to avoid sharp bends in the belts resulting from the weight of the hanging belts.

- If V-belts are stored on pegs, longer belts should be coiled in loops of suitable size to prevent distortion from the weight of the belt.

NOTE: Do not hang timing belts on pegs or nails. Timing belts should be stored in their original packages, avoiding any sharp bends or crimping.

- Do not twist, crimp, invert, or coil timing belts. Timing belts should not be bent tighter than the smallest recommended sprocket diameter for that cross section belt.

- Do not break matched sets—keep intact.

Storage On the Machine

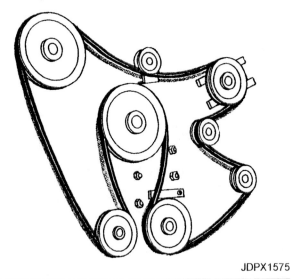

JDPX1575

Fig. 53 — Loosen All Belts if Stored on the Machine during Off Seasons

If a machine is stored for a long period, observe these rules:

- If belts are not to be removed, relieve belt tension by loosening all tighteners (Fig. 53). This is necessary to prevent the belt from "setting" or developing unequal stresses that might lead to early failure.

- If possible, remove all belts. Thoroughly clean them, then store in a cool, clean, dry place.

- If the belts are removed, coat sheave grooves with an anti-rust compound or grease prior to storage. Be sure to remove such rust preventives before installing the belts and starting the machine. Sheave grooves can also be protected with a section of discarded belt tied in place.

- Protect all movable or sliding parts of variable-speed drives by lubricating thoroughly to prevent corrosion due to moisture.

SUMMARY: MAINTENANCE OF V-BELTS

- *Listen for "ticking" sounds—they mean interference with belts.*

- *Replace all belts in a matched set at one time.*

- *V-belts stretch most during their first 24 hours of operation. Check tension and keep belts tight.*

- *Never attempt to correct belt slippage by using a belt dressing.*

- *If belts slip even when properly tensioned, check for overload, worn sheave grooves, or oil or grease on belts.*

- *Never pry a V-belt or force it into the sheave groove. Loosen the tightener before installing the belt.*

- *A belt which has operated while rolled over in the sheave groove is probably damaged—replace it.*

- *Store belts in a cool, dry place. If stored on a machine, be sure to relieve all belt tension.*

- *Never attempt to check or adjust belts while they are running.*

Maintenance of Flat Belts

Many of the maintenance tips for V-belts also apply to flat belts. Here are some other rules:

- Some flat belts, usually leather or canvas, may require *belt dressings* to prevent deterioration.

- Flat belts normally need *more tension* than V-belts.

- *Pulley alignment* is even more important with flat belts than for V-belts because flat belts can run off the pulley easier.

- *Never force* a belt off a moving pulley.

- *To install flat belts*, move the power unit forward, place the belt on the pulleys, and back up carefully to tighten the belt. Start the belt slowly to make sure it is running straight before increasing the speed.

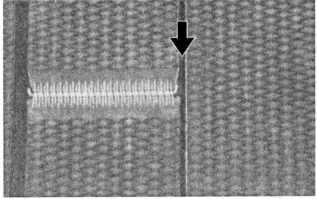

JDPX1576

Fig. 54 — Some Flat Belts are Spliced Together

- Flat belts that are spliced together, such as the bale-forming belts used on round balers, should be installed so that the trimmed end of the belts is trailing in the normal direction of travel (Fig. 54, arrow). Insert the splicing pin and bend the ends at 70 to 80 degree angle pointing toward the trimmed end of the belt (Fig. 54).

- Belt lacing tools and hardware are available for repairing broken flat belts. If the length of the belt being repaired is less than the dimension specified by the equipment manufacturer, a short piece of belt can be added to the belt. Splices within a belt should be at least 12 inches (305 mm) apart.

Maintenance of Synchronous (Timing) Belts

Many of the maintenance tips for V-belts also apply to timing belts. Here are some other rules:

When installing a timing belt, provisions must be made to adjust the belt center distance or change the idler position so that the belt can be slipped easily onto the drive. Never force or pry the belt onto a drive as this may cause internal damage to the belt tensile member.

Timing belts are sensitive to drive misalignment. In a misaligned drive, the load is being carried by only a small portion of the belt top width. This leads to inconsistent belt wear and premature tensile member failure due to the unequal tensile member loading. Misalignment should not exceed 1/16 in. (1.6 mm) per 12 in. (305 mm) of center distance.

Entrapment of debris in the drive can be more damaging to the timing belt drive than a V-belt drive. V-belt drives have a tendency to remove debris from the sheave grooves during drive operation. A timing belt has a tendency to pack debris into the sprocket grooves, causing improper belt tooth engagement and accelerating belt and sprocket wear. Adequate shielding must be provided for timing belt drives in environments where debris is likely.

Belt tension should be adjusted to the manufacturer's recommended value. **Too much tension** can impose excessive loads on the shafts and bearings and lead to reduced belt life.

Too little tension can result in the teeth climbing out of the sprocket grooves and the belt ratcheting (jumping teeth). This can lead to increased stresses on the belt teeth, accelerated tooth and sprocket wear, reduced belt life, and potential damage to the bearings and shafts.

Wear on V-Belts

First of all, remember that V-belts transmit power by friction and a *wedging* action between the sides of the belt and the inside walls of the sheave groove. This is where to look for signs of wear.

All belts and sheaves wear in use. Normal wear can be recognized as **even wear**—both on the belt and the sides of the sheave. It is **unusual wear** which you should look for and correct.

Many belts are reported as being defective but, upon closer examination, the failure has been traced to a bad sheave, misaligned drive or some other fault of a mechanical component of the machine. These problems were covered previously under "Maintenance of V-Belts."

Now let's look at failures of the belt itself.

EXAMPLES OF UNUSUAL V-BELT WEAR

Unusual V-belt wear is recognized by identifying signs of wear.

Some belts are ruined beyond use while others still have considerable service life left.

Base Cracking

JDPX1577

Fig. 55 — Base Cracking —Defective Belt

Excessive cross-cracking on the base of a belt having little or no side wear (Fig. 55, A) indicates the belt has been run a relatively short time and therefore must be defective. Except for the cracking, it is in nearly new condition. V-belts showing these wear signs are ruined beyond use.

If the sidewalls show three or four seasons use, the belt shouldn't be classified as being defective (Fig. 55, B). Actually, the cracks in the base of this belt show that it has been exposed to weather and the inner fabric is beginning to rot.

Fabric Rupture

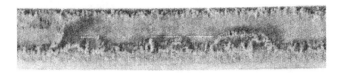

JDPX1578

Fig. 56 — Fabric Rupture—Damaged Belt

This belt (Fig. 56) is not defective. This type of rupture can be caused by operating a belt over badly worn sheaves, too much tension which forces the belt down into the grooves, or foreign objects falling into the sheave groove while the drive is operating.

In these cases, check the condition of the sheaves. Check the belt tension and adjust to the recommended value. Avoid prying the belts onto the sheaves.

Cover Tear

JDPX1579

Fig. 57 — Cover Tear—Damaged Belt

Fig. 57 is an example of damage caused by the belt accidentally coming into contact with some part of the machine, tearing the cover. It is no fault of the belt or its construction.

In many cases, such failure is due to belts running too loose, allowing them to "throw-out" centrifugally so that they rub on parts of the machine. Proper belt tension prevents this from happening.

NOTE: A slight raveling of the belt covering at the splice does not indicate premature failure. The raveling should be cut off if the covering peels at the lap.

Spin Burn

JDPX1580

Fig. 58 — Spin Burn—Damaged Belt

The general appearance of the belt in Fig. 58 indicates that it has been properly tensioned. Apparently the driven sheave stalled and the drive sheave continued to run, resulting in a burned area, ruining the belt beyond use.

Prevent drives from locking by checking the tension of any belts in the drive train. Avoid overloading and plugging the machine. Never attempt to run a plugged machine without first cleaning it out. Lubricate the machine at the specified intervals to prevent bearing seizure.

Slip Burn

JDPX1581

Fig. 59 — Slip Burn—Damaged Belt

The belt in Fig. 59 has been ruined beyond use by being operated too loose. The belt slipped under load, and when it finally grabbed, it snapped.

In these cases, check belt tension and check belts for wear more often. Turn drives over by hand to make sure they are free. Clear the machine of any loads before stopping to avoid overloading the drives when starting up again.

Gouged Edge

JDPX1582

Fig. 60 — Gouged Edge—Damaged Belt

Except for the gouged edge, the entire circumference of the belt in Fig. 60 is in new condition. Damage was caused by either a damaged sheave or interference with some part of the machine. This belt still has considerable service life remaining.

In this case, check the condition of the sheaves. Make sure the belt does not rub on any part of the machine while operating.

Ruptured Cords

JDPX1583

Fig. 61 — Ruptured Cords —Damaged Belt

The belt shown in Fig. 61 has ruptured cords and is ruined beyond use. Damage may have been caused by foreign material between the sheave and belt or too much tension.

In these cases, clean foreign material from the sheaves and check that screens and shields are in place. Check belt tension and adjust to the recommended value.

Worn Sides

JDPX1584

Fig. 62 — Worn Sides —Damaged Belt

The belt shown in Fig. 62 is a typical example of a badly worn belt resulting from long operation without enough tension. The sides are worn and the entire circumference is slightly burned. Rapid sidewall wear may also be the result of worn or damaged sheaves, using the wrong belt cross section or type, excessive oil or grease, use of belt dressing, excessive heat, or operating in an abrasive environment.

To prevent this, check belt tension more often and adjust to recommended value. Also check the sheaves for wear or damage. If belt-to-sheave groove mismatch is suspected, belt and sheave groove gauges can be used to check dimensions. Never attempt to correct belt slippage by using a belt dressing.

Wear Due to Misaligned Drive

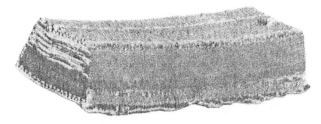

JDPX1585

Fig. 63 — Wear Due to Misaligned Drive—Damaged Belt

The belt shown in Fig. 63 has been operating on a misaligned drive. Notice how both plies of the cover band have been completely worn off of one sidewall while the other side of the belt shows normal wear.

To prevent this, check the sheaves for misalignment.

DEFECTIVE V-BELTS

While the preceding examples illustrated only one belt (Base Cracking—Defective Belt) that can be termed **defective** (Fig. 55), some other types of defective belts not easily shown by photographs are as follows:

Excessive Stretch

A belt that stretches excessively is one that stretches beyond the limit of the tightener adjustment provided to take up normal belt stretch. This will usually occur within the warranty period.

Lumpy Belts

Lumpy belts usually occur and are more noticeable on variable speed drives and other high speed belt installations. The result is excessive vibration.

Internal Cord Failure

Failure of one or more of the internal tension cords will result in the belt rolling over on the sheaves. (Cords can be broken by prying a new belt over sheaves.)

Improper Length

It is possible for belts either too long or too short to be shipped accidentally in repair parts orders. Such belts would not pass the line run-in for new machines at the factory.

Wear on Banded V-Belts

Banded V-belts have some wear problems which are unique so let's look at them in a separate story.

One Belt Riding Outside Sheave Grooves

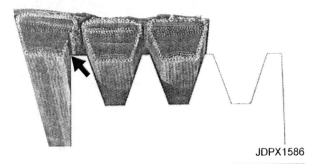

JDPX1586

Fig. 64 — Banded V-Belt Riding Outside of Sheave Grooves

Trouble Area and Observation	Possible Cause	Remedy
Banded belt with one strand riding outside sheave grooves. There is a distinct groove in sidewall of outside belt (Fig. 64).	Possible misalignment, lack of tension or foreign object forced belt from sheave grooves.	Properly align drive, adjust tension, and remove any interference.

NOTE: *If the above belt were permitted to run in this position, progressive failure would result as shown next in Figs. 65 and 66.*

Separation of One Belt from Band

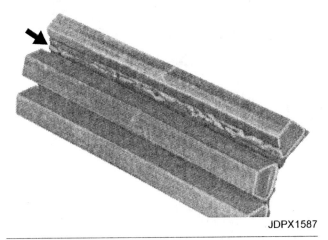

JDPX1587

Fig. 65 — Separation of One Belt from Band

Trouble Area and Observation	Possible Cause	Remedy
Outside belt and belt adjacent to it have started to separate from tie band (Fig. 65).	Banded belt has jumped one groove, forcing outside belt out of sheave. Improper tension, misalignment, or a foreign object struck belt and forced it from normal path.	Replace complete banded belt and seat properly in aligned grooves. Tension properly.

Separation of All Belts from Band

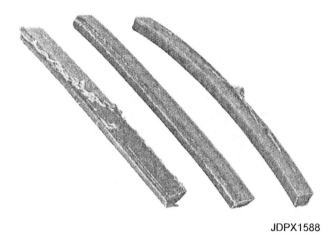

JDPX1588

Fig. 66 — Separation of All Belts from Band

Trouble Area and Observation	Possible Cause	Remedy
Belts have separated completely from tie band (Fig. 66).	Riding outside of sheave grooves.	Proper maintenance of drive and installation of new belt.

Short Belt Life—Bottom of Belts Cracking

JDPX1589

Fig. 67 — Short Belt Life—Bottom Of Belts Cracking

Trouble Area and Observation	Possible Cause	Remedy
Bottom of belts cracking (Fig. 67).	Belt running on too-small sheaves. Belt slipping causes heat build-up and gradual hardening of undercord.	Consider minimum diameters for drives, drive and idler sheaves, and pulleys. Check belt tension.

Short Belt Life—Top of Band Frayed

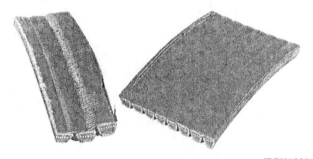

JDPX1590

Fig. 68 — Short Belt Life—Top Of Band Frayed Or Damaged

Trouble Area and Observation	Possible Cause	Remedy
Top of tie band frayed or damaged (Fig. 68).	Obstruction on machine interfering with normal operation of belt.	Realign drive and remove obstruction.

Short Belt Life—Band Separating from Belts

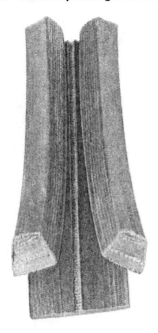

JDPX1591

Fig. 69 — Short Belt Life—Band Separating From Belts

Trouble Area and Observation	Possible Cause	Remedy
Tie band separating from belts (Fig. 69).	Worn sheaves or incorrect groove spacing.	Gauge sheave grooves and replace with new standard groove sheaves.

Short Belt Life—Holes or Blisters in Tie Band

JDPX1592

Fig. 70 — Short Belt Life—Holes Or Blisters In Tie Band

Trouble Area and Observation	Possible Cause	Remedy
Large holes or blisters appear on tie band (Fig. 70).	Trash and foreign material accumulating between belts.	Install drive shields.

Wear on Flat Belts

Common wear on flat belts is explained next.

Flat Belt Tears

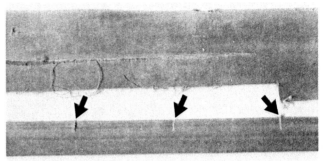

JDPX1593

Fig. 71 — Flat Belt Tears—Damaged Belt

An improperly aligned tightener pulley caused this drive flat belt to climb the inner edge of the engine drive pulley, tearing the edge of the belt (Fig. 71). One of these tears eventually caused the belt to tear completely through.

Check belt and pulley alignment to prevent unnecessary wear on the edges of the belt.

Flat Belt Burn

JDPX1594

Fig. 72 — Flat Belt Burn—Damaged Belt

The shiny appearance and the badly burned area (Fig. 72) were caused by operating this drive belt too loose. Note the notch in the edge of the belt (arrow) where it slid sideways against the flange of the drive pulley while slipping and burned the center section. Similar damage can result from attempting to start a machine without first cleaning it out and removing the load.

Check belt tension periodically to prevent this type of belt damage.

Wear on Synchronous Belts

Synchronous (timing) belts have some wear problems, which are unique. Let's look at failures of synchronous belts.

Belt Tensile Break

Damage to the belt tensile member can result in belt separation under load. A common cause of belt tensile member damage is improper belt handling and storage prior to installation.

Timing belts should not be twisted, crimped or inverted. Belts should not be bent tighter than the smallest recommended sprocket diameter for that cross section belt. Under no circumstances should the belt be forced or pried onto a drive. Debris or a foreign objects in the drive can also damage the tensile member and cause the belt to fracture.

Belt Edge Wear

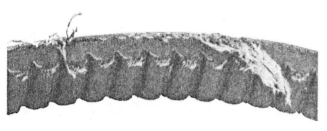

JDPX1595

Fig. 73 — Frayed Edges

Excessive belt edge wear (Fig. 73) is caused by belt misalignment, rough or damaged flange surface, insufficient belt tension, or belt rubbing against drive guard or bracket.

Check belt and sprocket alignment to prevent wear on the edges of the belt. Check belt tension more often. Make sure that the belt does not rub on any part of the machine while operating.

Drive Belt Disintegration

JDPX1596

Fig. 74 — Timing Belt Disintegration

Improper contact of the belt teeth in the sprockets can cause premature wear of the timing belt (Fig. 74). Insufficient belt tension can result in belt ratcheting (jumping teeth), leading to rapid tooth and sprocket wear. A misaligned drive does not allow equal distribution of the load across the entire tooth width, resulting in excessive wear of the portion of teeth carrying the higher load. Improper tooth contact can also be caused by worn, damaged or rough sprocket teeth. Similar belt damage can result from using a belt with incorrect tooth profile for the sprockets.

Check belt tension and adjust to value recommended by the manufacturer. Check belt and sprocket alignment to prevent unnecessary wear of the belt teeth. Replace worn or damaged sprockets. Use the proper belt/sprocket combination.

Tooth Shear

JDPX1597

Fig. 75 — Timing Belt Teeth Sheared

Excessive shock load caused the teeth to shear from this belt (Fig. 75). Excessive shock load can be the result of insufficient belt tension, worn sprockets, misaligned drive, incorrect belt profile for the sprocket, or having less than six teeth in mesh with the sprocket.

Check for binding or improperly installed drive components that could cause a violent engagement of the drive sheave. Check belt tension and belt alignment more often.

Maintenance of Serpentine Belts

Serpentine belts are generally longer-lasting than most other belts. The automatic tensioner and belt work together with the drive pulley. The driven pulleys (sometimes called companion pulleys) drive all the related systems.

Generally, the automatic tensioner is designed to last the life of the serpentine belt. Most often, the tensioner and belt should be changed together when maintenance is required. Visual inspection for cracks and chunks missing determine when these components should be changed (Fig. 76). Often manufacturer recommend maintenance intervals by hours of service or millage on a vehicle odometer.

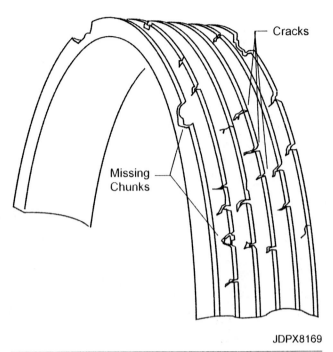

Cracks

Missing Chunks

JDPX8169

Fig. 76 — Failing Serpentine Belt

Replacing Serpentine Belts

Serpentine belts are generally very long and are installed over and under number of pulleys. Each these pulleys typically drives a specific device. These systems always have an automatic tensioner. The tension must be released while removing the damaged belt and while installing the replacement belt.

 CAUTION: The automatic tensioner is a spring loaded device that stores a significant amount of energy. Fingers can become entangled and crushed under the pressure.

Always refer to the pulley configuration chart to find out the correct belt routing. This chart is found in the service manual or on a decal near the serpentine belt system. The spring load on the tensioner can be released with a wrench, ratchet handle or special tensioner tool, depending on the manufacturer's design. With one hand, relieve the tension and with the other hand, carefully remove the damaged belt. When the damaged belt is removed, gradually move the tensioner back into the original position.

Install the replacement belt by moving the tensioner to a position that allows the replacement belt to fit into place. Move the tension with one hand and carefully route the replacement belt with the other hand. When the belt is properly routed, carefully and gradually allow the tensioner to take up the slack.

Troubleshooting Belt Drives

The following troubleshooting chart is designed to give a general guide to diagnosing problems with belt drives.

BELT DRIVE TROUBLESHOOTING CHART		
Problem	**Possible Cause**	**Remedy**
Rapid V-belt wear	Rubbing belt guard	Check guard clearance
	Sheave misalignment	Correct sheave alignment
	Worn or damaged sheave grooves	Check groove sidewalls, replace sheaves
	Wrong belt cross section or type	Check belt and sheave dimensions, replace belt
	Sheave diameter too small	Use larger diameter sheave
	Improper V-belt installation, belts pried over sheaves	Determine how belt was installed (Replace belts, do not pry belts over sheaves)
	Overloaded drive	Reduce load
	Belts improperly stored or in storage too long	Use new set of V-belts
	Mismatched belts	Replace with matched set of belts
	Replacing one belt in multiple-belt drive	Replace complete set of V-belts
	V-belt slipping	Increase tension
V-belts turned over in sheave groove	Broken cords in V-belts, belts pried over sheaves	Determine how belt was installed (Replace belts, do not pry belts over sheaves)
	Overloaded drive	Reduce loads
	Defective cord construction in V-belt	Check for narrow spot in belt, replace belts
	Impulse loads	Use banded V-belts or spring-loaded idlers
V-belt slippage	Lack of tension	Increase tension
	Overloaded drive	Reduce loads
	Sheave worn, belt bottoming in groove (Shiny sheave groove bottom)	Replace sheave
	Sheave grooves too wide, belts bottoming in grooves	Use belt with larger cross section or replace sheave
	Oily drive conditions	Correct the oil or grease condition
V-belt squeal	Lack of tension	Increase tension
	Overloaded drive	Reduce loads
	Insufficient arc of contact	Increase center distance between sheaves

BELT DRIVE TROUBLESHOOTING CHART (CONTINUED)		
Problem	**Possible Cause**	**Remedy**
Checked or cracked V-belts	Belt slippage	Increase belt tension
	Excessive heat	Provide adequate ventilation and check belt tension
Repeated V-belt fracture	Shock loads	Increase V-belt tension. Heavier drive may be required
	Heavy starting loads	Increase V-belt tension. Heavier drive may be required
	Improper V-belt installation, belts pried over sheaves	Determine how belt was installed. (Replace belts, do not pry belts over sheaves)
Flat belt drive operating improperly	Insufficient tension causing belt slippage	Increase tension
	Pulley with excessive crown	Remove excessive crown
	Center distance too long (Belts run of pulley)	Use shorter center distance between pulleys
	Slippage on flat pulleys	Use shorter center distance or replace flat belt with V-belt
	Excessive shock loads (Belts run off pulley)	Use V-belts
Synchronous belt noise or vibration	Misaligned drive	Correct drive alignment
	Incorrect belt tension	Adjust tension to recommended value
	Belt speed too high	Redesign drive for slower belt speed or use properly rated belt
	Incorrect belt profile for sprocket	Use proper belt/sprocket combination
	Sprocket diameter smaller than specified minimum	Redesign drive using larger diameter sprockets
	Overloaded drive	Reduce the load. Heavier drive may be required
Synchronous belt edge wear	Sprocket flange damaged	Replace the sprocket
	Belt too wide	Use proper width belt or sprocket
	Belt tension too low	Adjust belt tension to recommended value
	Drive misalignment causing improper tracking	Correct drive alignment
	Belt rubbing drive guard or support bracket	Check guard clearance
Synchronous belt tensile break	Shock loads	Redesign drive for increased capacity

BELT DRIVE TROUBLESHOOTING CHART (CONTINUED)		
Problem	**Possible Cause**	**Remedy**
	Improper belt handling and storage prior to installation	Store belts in their original package (Avoid any sharp bends or crimping)
	Forcing belt onto drive during installation	Determine how belt was installed (Do not pry belt over sprockets)
	Debris or foreign object in drive	Remove debris and check drive guard
Rapid serpentine belt wear	Misalignment	Correct alignment
	Worn or damaged pulley grooves	Check grooves and replace as needed
	Wrong belt	Replace belt
	Wrong pullies	Replace with correct pullies
	Overloaded drive	Reduce load
	Belt improperly stored or stored too long	Replace belt
	Belt slippage	Replace automatic tensioner
Serpentine belt slippage	Lack of tension	Replace automatic tensioner
	Overloaded drive	Reduce load
Serpentine belt squeal	Wrong belt	Replace belt
Cracks in Serpentine belt	Belt in service too long	Replace belt

Test Yourself

QUESTIONS

1. What are the four basic types of belts?

2. How are V-belts driven?

   a. From the bottom of the sheave groove.

   b. From the sides of the sheave groove.

   c. Both of the above.

3. True or false? "When a V-belt runs around its sheaves, the bottom of the belt stretches."

4. Why do pulleys for flat belts have a crown or raised center for the belt surface?

5. If the drive pulley has a diameter of 12 in. (304.8 mm) while the driven pulley has a diameter of 6 in. (152.4 mm), which shaft will turn twice as fast as the other?

6. How is variable speed obtained in a belt drive?

7. True or false? "An idler pulley functions best when run on the slack side of the belt."

8. True or false? "As a general rule, V-belts can tolerate sheave misalignment up to 1/8 in. (3.2 mm) per 12 in. (305 mm) of shaft center distance."

9. True or false? "Always replace all belts at the same time on a multiple-belt drive."

10. If a belt squeals, what are the two most likely causes?

11. True or false? "A good belt dressing is the best way to reduce slippage of V-belts."

12. When a machine is stored, how should the belts be tensioned?

13. True or false? "The only way to assure that a serpentine belt is properly tensioned is to use a belt tension gauge."

14. What type of belt requires an automatic tensioner?

CHAINS

Introduction

Chain drives are a form of flexible gearing. The chain is like an endless gear rack, while the sprockets are similar to pinions or driven gears.

Chain drives are similar to belt drives except that they are less flexible. They can generally manage greater loads than belts. Chains carry loads without the slippage that is typical in many belt drives applications.

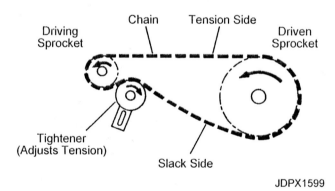

JDPX1599

Fig. 1 — Parts of a Chain Drive

Chain drives consist of one or more **sprockets** and an endless **chain** (Fig. 1).

In some situations, belts and drives perform equally well. This is especially true when comparing timing belts to chains (Fig. 2). In these cases, choosing one over the other is decided by considering factors such as maintenance costs, part availability etc.

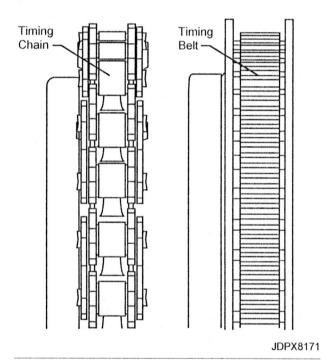

JDPX8171

Fig. 2 — Chain-to-belt Comparison

An example of an area where chain and belt performance tend to overlap is in engine timing. Both chains and timing belts perform equally well in engine timing applications. They last about the same amount of time but belts are often less costly parts. For this reason, timing belts are generally used today where chains were used in the past.

Principles of Chain Drives

- Chain drives are normally used to transmit power from one rotating shaft to another.

- The links of the chain mesh with the teeth of the sprockets and maintain a positive speed ratio between the driving and driven sprockets.

- Sprockets connected to the same side of a chain revolve in the same direction. If connected on reverse sides, they revolve in opposite directions.

- Sprockets for roller chain drives must have at least twelve teeth to avoid excessive wear, noise, and vibration.

- If the chain has an even number of pitches (spaces between links), the sprockets have an odd number of teeth, and vice versa. This prevents a single link from contacting the same tooth each time, causing uneven wear and vibration.

- A small sprocket causes sharper bending of the chain and more wear.

- Short links bend less and should be used on smaller sprockets.

- Chains may be installed in single or multiple strands, depending on the load.

- Chain slack must be adjusted from time to time by moving one of the main sprockets or using a chain tightener (Fig. 1).

- Horizontal chain drives should have the slack side on the bottom if possible.

- Tighteners or idlers should be on the slack side of the chain.

ADVANTAGES OF CHAINS (AS COMPARED WITH BELTS)

- Chain drives do not slip or creep as do flat or V-belt drives. As a result, chains maintain a positive speed ratio between the driving and the driven shafts and are more efficient since no power is lost due to slippage.

- Chain drives are more compact than belt drives. For a given capacity, a chain will be narrower than a belt, and the sprockets will be smaller in diameter than pulleys.

- Chains are easier to install.

- Chains can operate at higher temperatures than belts.

- Chain drives are usually more practical for very low speeds.

- Chains do not deteriorate due to age, oil, grease, or sunlight but they may rust if not protected.

DISADVANTAGES OF CHAIN DRIVES

- Chain drives are fairly noisy.

- Chains usually require frequent lubrication.

- Most chains will tolerate very little misalignment.

- Chains cannot normally be used where the drive must slip. (There are exceptions.)

Uses of Chains

The three basic jobs of chains are:

- **Transmitting power**

- **Converting motion**

- **Timing or synchronizing**

JDPX1600

Fig. 3 — Transmitting Power

In TRANSMITTING POWER, chains and sprockets are used as flexible gearing to transmit torque from one rotating shaft to another (Fig. 3).

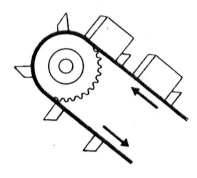

JDPX1601

Fig. 4 — Converting Motion (Conveying)

In CONVERTING MOTION, chains are used to convey materials by sliding, pushing, pulling, or carrying (Fig. 4).

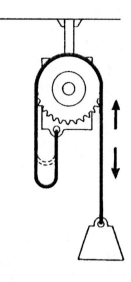

JDPX1602

Fig. 5 — Timing or Synchronizing

In TIMING or SYNCHRONIZING, chains are used as devices to synchronize movements such as valve timing in engines or raising loads on an overhead chain hoist (Fig. 5).

Types of Chains

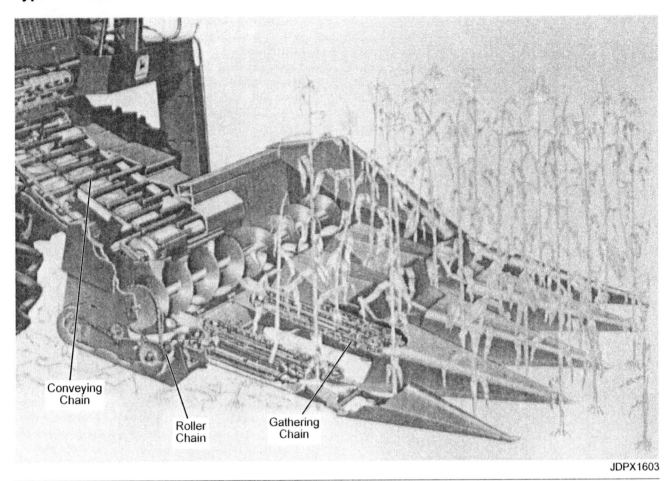

Conveying Chain

Roller Chain

Gathering Chain

JDPX1603

Fig. 6 — Types of Chains

There are two major groups of chains that are used in powered mechanical applications. They are the agricultural and precision groups.

The agricultural machine chain is used mainly to convey or carry material and not to transmit power. Two types of agricultural chain are the CA550 and CA555. The CA550 chain is a standard conveying chain. The CA555 is a special corn head gathering chain (Fig. 6).

There are six basic types of precision chains used in chain drives:

- **Roller chain**
- **Rollerless chain**
- **Silent chain**
- **Detachable link chain**
- **Pintle chain**
- **Block chain**

Now let's look at each one in detail.

ROLLER CHAIN

JDPX1604

Fig. 7 — Roller Chain

Roller chains are widely used for moderate speeds and heavy loads, and where average wear is expected. Standard pitch chains are used for speeds up to 4500 feet per minute (1370 m/min), while extended pitches are designed for slower speeds. See page 6 for an explanation of "pitch."

Construction

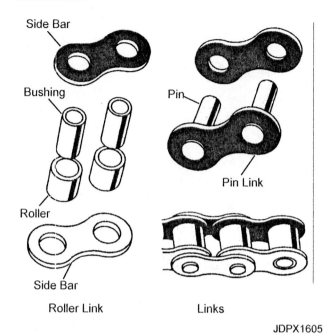

Fig. 8 — Construction of Roller Chain

Standard roller chain is made up of alternate roller links and pin links (Fig. 8). Roller links have two side bars, two bushings, and two rollers, while pin links have two side bars and two pins.

The pins and bushings provide the bearing surfaces for the chain links to hinge or articulate over the sprockets. The rollers provide smooth rolling action as the chain enters and leaves the sprocket.

The pin forms one part of the roller chain joint. In addition, the pin connects one link to another and is the shear member between each set of side bars. To prevent rapid chain wear, the pin must be prevented from rotating in the outer side bars. This is usually accomplished by a press fit (riveting) between the pin and side bars or by mechanical locking devices.

A removable pin link may be used for connecting the chain ends, although the complete chain may be joined by removable pins. A fastener, such as a retaining clip or cotter pin, will be used to lock the removable pins in the side bar.

The chain bushing forms the other part of the roller chain joint. The bushings are locked laterally and are prevented from rotating in the side bars by press fits between the bushings and side bars or by mechanical locks. The bushing outside diameter also provides the bearing surface for the chain roller.

The side bars of the roller chain are the tensile members connecting the chain joints. The side bars also determine the pitch (or angle) of the chain. Double pitch or extended pitch roller chain has the same parts as standard-pitch chain, but the side plates have twice the pitch (See Fig. 11 on page 6). Double pitch chains are lighter in weight and less expensive.

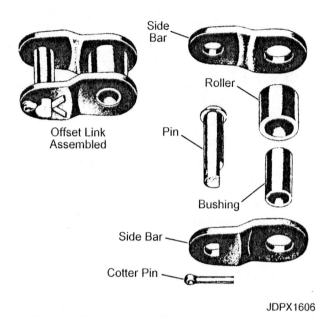

Fig. 9 — Roller Chain with Offset Links

Some roller chains have *offset* links, which are roller links and pin links combined (Fig. 9). The offset link is often used to connect chains where an odd number of links are required.

An offset link can be removed to adjust the chain length to compensate for chain pitch elongation resulting from wear.

JDPX1607

Fig. 10 — Roller Chain with Multiple Strands

Roller chains are available in double, triple, and other multiple strands as shown in (Fig. 10).

Operation

As the roller chain goes around the sprocket, it bends or hinges at each link end. The bushing turns on the pin, while the roller contacts the sprocket teeth and guides the link into place, absorbing most of the friction by a rolling motion.

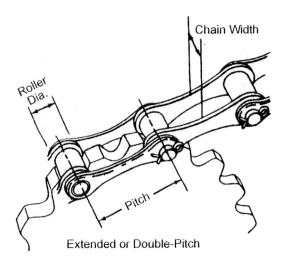

Extended or Double-Pitch

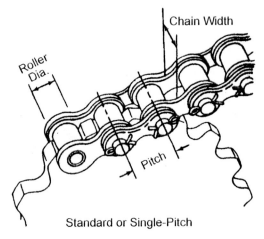

Standard or Single-Pitch

JDPX1608

Fig. 11 — Roller Chain Pitch, Width, and Roller Diameters

The pitch of a roller chain is the distance between the centers of the rollers (Fig. 11), which is established by the chain side bars. Standard or *single* pitch is shown at the bottom, while extended or *double* pitch is shown at the top. As we said earlier, double pitch chains are cheaper but should only be used for light loads transmitted at low speeds.

Chain width is the distance between the inside edges of the side bars.

Roller diameter is the width across each roller in the chain.

Roller chains are numbered 40, 50, 60 etc. to match their sizes. The following chain size chart shows the standard chain numbers and what they mean in terms of pitch, width, and roller diameter.

SILENT CHAIN

JDPX1610

Fig. 13 — Silent Chain

STANDARD ROLLER CHAIN SIZES (NEW CHAINS)				
Chain No.	150 Chain No.	Pitch in. (mm)	Width in. (mm)	Roller Diameter in. (mm)
40	08A	1/2 (12.7)	5/16 (7.9)	5/16 (7.9)
50	10A	5/8 (15.8)	3/8 (9.5)	0.400 (10.1)
60	12A	3/4 (19)	1/2 (12.7)	15/32 (11.9)
80	16A	1 (25.4)	5/8 (15.8)	5/8 (15.8)
100	20A	1-1/4 (31.7)	3/4 (19)	3/4 (19)
120	24A	1-1/2 (38.1)	1 (25.4)	7/8 (22.2)
140	28A	1-3/4 (44.4)	1 (25.4)	1 (25.4)
160	32A	2 (50.8)	1-1/4 (31.7)	1-1/8 (28.5)
180	*	2-1/4 (57.1)	1-13/32 (35.7)	1-13/32 (35.7)
200	40A	2-1/2 (63.5)	1-1/2 (38.1)	1-9/16 (39.6)
*No. 150 Number				

Silent chain (Fig. 13) is designed for quiet operation. It will run at high speeds—over 4500 feet per minute (1370 meters per minute)—with little noise or vibration. This chain is often used for valve timing in automotive engines.

ROLLERLESS CHAIN

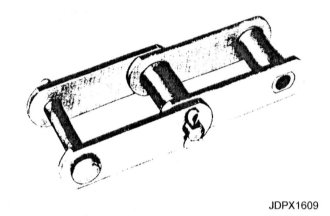

JDPX1609

Fig. 12 — Rollerless Chain

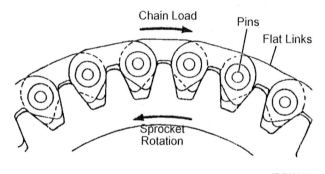

JDPX1611

Fig. 14 — How a Silent Chain Engages the Sprocket

Rollerless chain (Fig. 12) is used for lower speeds and where chain wear is not critical. A series of one-piece cast links are fastened with side bars and pins.

In operation, the chain links contact the sprocket teeth and hinge to follow the circle of the sprocket. However, there is no rolling action in the chain; the only motion is the hinging which takes place inside the cast bushing or barrel of the link.

Silent chain is a series of flat metal links with a tooth shape at each end, connected by pins to form a flexible, continuous chain (Fig. 14).

The sprockets are similar to gears in appearance and design. The chain passes over the face of the sprocket like a belt and the teeth of the sprocket do not project through the chain. This causes the links to enter and leave the sprocket in a smooth, orderly way.

The chain links are small in proportion to the chain's strength so it can be used on smaller sprockets. Some silent chains are made with links having teeth on both sides so that over-and-under serpentine drives can be used.

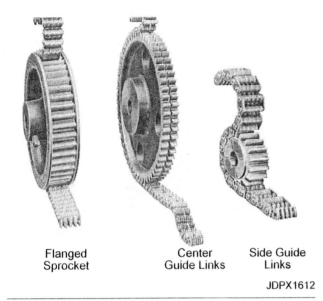

Flanged Sprocket | Center Guide Links | Side Guide Links

JDPX1612

Fig. 15— Three Ways of Retaining Silent Chains

Silent chains can be retained on their sprockets in any of the three ways shown in Fig. 15.

DETACHABLE LINK CHAIN

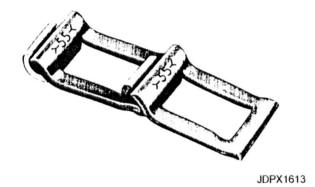

JDPX1613

Fig. 16 — Detachable Link Chain

This is a simple, cheap chain for slow speeds and very light loads. It is sometimes called "plain chain."

The links are of steel or cast iron and are easily replaced. One end of the link is the hook end and the other the bar end.

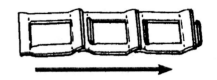

JDPX1614

Fig. 17 — Detachable Link Chains are Directional

Most chains can be driven in either direction, but detachable link chains are an exception (Fig. 17).

PINTLE CHAIN

JDPX1615

Fig. 18 — Pintle Chain

Pintle chain (Fig. 18) is used for slow speeds where abrasive materials and exposure to weather are critical. Link pitches from 1-1/2 to 6 in. (38 to 150 mm) allow it to be used on a variety of conveyors. Speeds are usually 450 rpm or less, while loads are fairly light.

The chain is made up of a series of malleable iron links joined together by pins. The connecting pins are locked into the open end of the link and will not turn. As the chain forms around the sprocket, it hinges in the barrel, rotating around its fixed pin.

BLOCK CHAIN

JDPX1616

Fig. 19 — Block Chain

This chain is a series of cast blocks joined by side bars and pins (Fig. 19). It is used for conveying small materials and may be equipped with pusher bars.

The chain is constructed by coupling two links with coupling pins or rivets which are securely locked against turning in the outside link. The coupling pins or rivets are free to turn in the smooth hardened bores of the bushings.

As the chain forms around the sprocket, hinging action takes place inside the bushing.

OTHER CHAINS

Here are some other chains which are less common:

Bushing Chains—all-steel chain for rugged conveying jobs. Made up of alternate straight side bar inner links and straight bar outer links. The inner link is made of two side bars and two hardened steel barrels or bushings.

Straight Sidebar Chain—a simpler version of the bushing chain, using only two side bars and using rollers at the link pins.

Leaf Chain—uses tension links for lifting and counter-balancing chains; very high-strength.

Side Bow Chain—a standard roller chain with special pin links which allow side flexing for curved or twisting conveyor lines.

Plate Top Chain—large plates for conveying are fastened to tops of roller links. (Larger version is used as tracks on crawler tractors.)

Flexible Chain—This chain replaces belts in some applications. The metal slats form teeth as they operate. Variable-speed drive is also an option with this chain.

Saw Chain This is a special chain for cutting wood.

O-Ring Sealed Chain—O-Ring sealed chains are gaining popularity in environments that are highly abrasive to unprotected chains.

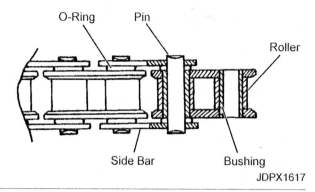

JDPX1617

Fig. 20 — O-Ring Sealed Chain

The O-rings, located between the side bars (Fig. 20), seal in the lubricant between the pin and bushing. The O-rings also prevent water, abrasives and other contaminants from entering the pin and bushing bearing area.

The sealed-in lubricant allows the pin and bushing to articulate with very little friction, virtually eliminating internal wear of the pins and bushings and greatly increasing the service life of the chain. The reduced pin-to-bushing friction also enables the O-ring sealed chain to operate in high speed applications more efficiently than a conventional unsealed roller chain.

Drive Arrangements

The relative position of sprockets in chain drives is carefully planned to get maximum life from the drive.

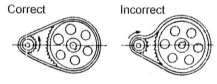

JDPX1618

Fig. 21 — Close Center Horizontal Drives

On close-center horizontal drives (Fig. 21), the rotation of the sprockets should be such that the slack resulting from wear is on the lower strand. This will prevent chain pinching between sprockets.

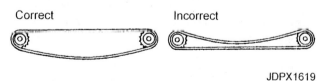

JDPX1619

Fig. 22 — Extremely Long Center Horizontal Drives

On extremely long center drives (Fig. 22), the rotation of the sprockets should be such that accumulating slack will tend to fall away from the tight strand, rather than fall onto it. Interference between strands could cause premature failure.

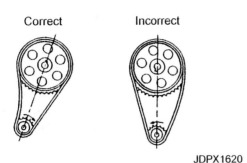

Correct   Incorrect

JDPX1620

Fig. 23 — Vertical Drives with Small Sprocket on Bottom

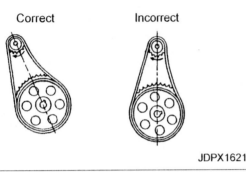

Correct   Incorrect

JDPX1621

Fig. 24 — Vertical Drives with Small Sprocket on Top

Avoid vertical drives wherever possible (Figs. 23 and 24), particularly with the small sprocket on the bottom. If possible, design on an incline, so that the slack will fall into the driven sprocket, rather than away from it. This will help avoid sprocket misengagement.

The most desirable arrangement of the chain drive is horizontal with the slack side strand on the bottom (Fig. 21, left). Horizontal drives with the slack side strand on the top and vertical drives may require some type of chain tightener to adjust the slack side tension to provide the correct chain/sprocket mesh. A minimum 120 degrees of chain wrap on the smaller sprocket should be maintained.

For normal chain drives, the center-to-center shaft distances should be between 30 and 50 pitches. A recommended minimum center distance is the sum of the diameter of the larger sprocket and one-half the diameter of the smaller sprocket. Center distances less than 20 pitches should be avoided because the drive will tend to run hot and wear rapidly. Center distances greater than 80 pitches should also be avoided because chain wear will cause excessive chain sag, and a small misalignment can cause the chain to run off the sprockets.

Location of Chain Tighteners

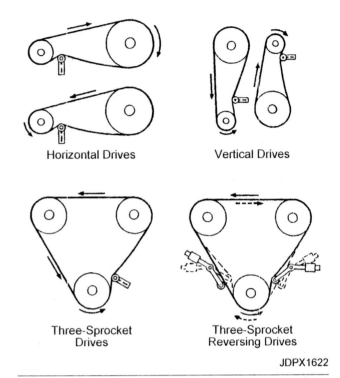

Horizontal Drives   Vertical Drives

Three-Sprocket Drives   Three-Sprocket Reversing Drives

JDPX1622

Fig. 25 — Location of Chain Tighteners

On drives where it is not practical to have adjustable centers, or where longer center distances might cause the slack side of the chain to strike an obstruction or "whip" too much, the installation of a chain tightener is recommended(Fig. 25).

If an idler sprocket is used as a chain tightener, it should be no smaller than the drive sprocket and should engage the chain in the slack span. The idler sprocket should engage at least three chain pitches, and there should be at least three chain pitches between the engagement points of the idle and the drive sprockets.

CONVEYOR AND ELEVATOR CHAIN TIGHTENERS

Most conveyors and elevators control chain tension through the use of a tightening device.

Following are typical tightening devices:

- **Screw Tightener**
- **Gravity Tightener**
- **Spring Tightener**
- **Catenary Tightener**

Adjusting to the proper chain tension can often correct such conveyor problems as surging and buckling. With proper tension, the wear on chain and sprockets resulting from improper tooth engagement and from lateral trailing of the chain can be drastically reduced. Tighteners are also useful for equalizing the tension in two or more strands of chain applied to a single conveyor system.

Proper conveyor and elevator chain tension should:

- Allow for chain elongation caused by both chain wear (progressive) and elastic stretch (intermittent).

- Be based on operating or running conditions (not static conditions).

- Avoid any static overloading.

- Provide temporary chain slack for coupling and maintenance.

- Use a positive tightening system.

- Involve frequent inspection and resetting of take-ups.

Tightening devices can be either manual, such as the screw type, or automatic, such as the gravity type or spring type. Some applications may require both.

Screw Tightener

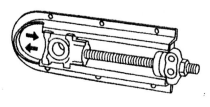

JDPX1623

Fig. 26 — Screw Tightener

A screw tightener (Fig. 26) is used where periodic manual adjustments are sufficient.

Gravity Tightener

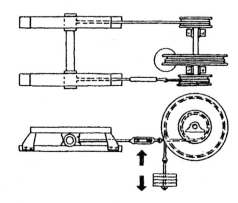

JDPX1624

Fig. 27 — Gravity Tightener

Gravity tighteners (Fig. 27) are used where constant adjustment is desirable to compensate for chain wear.

Spring Tightener

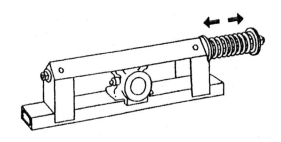

JDPX1625

Fig. 28 — Spring Tightener

Spring Tighteners (Fig. 28) are especially useful for shock loading conditions. Because of limited travel of the spring, manual adjustments are also necessary.

Catenary Tightener

JDPX1626

Fig. 29 — Catenary Tightener

Catenary tighteners (Fig. 29) are useful in long conveyors where the catenary can follow the drive sprocket, relieving chain tension throughout the rest of the conveyor. The catenary provides "automatic" tensioning of the chain.

Matching Chains and Sprockets

Replacement chains will operate on the same sprocket only if these three dimensions are the same:

- Chain pitch
- Roller or bushing diameter
- Inside chain width

These three dimensions are described on page 6.

When replacing chains, all three dimensions must match. Otherwise, the sprockets must also be replaced.

Be careful when assembling parts from another chain into one already in use. Poor fits can shorten chain life. Normally, this is done only in an emergency until normal repairs can be made.

When two or more chains operate side by side, the total assembled chain pitch must be the same. If not, the shorter strand will be overloaded, or the chain can become twisted when engaging the sprockets. To avoid trouble, replace multiple strands as a complete unit.

"HUNTING TOOTH" SPROCKET DESIGN (DOUBLE-PITCH CHAINS)

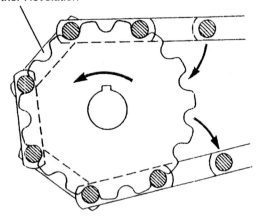

JDPX1627

Fig. 30 — "Hunting Tooth" Sprocket Design (Double-Pitch Chains)

The rate of wear in sprocket teeth can be retarded by the use of double-cut sprockets with the "hunting tooth" design (Fig. 30).

This arrangement provides an "extra set" of teeth, as well as an odd number of teeth, so that each tooth *contacts the chain only every other revolution*. Less contact results in proportionately less wear.

Obviously, this can only be used with double-pitch chains. The space available for the extra set of teeth must be adequate to provide tooth sections of proper strength.

RELATIVE SPEED OF SPROCKETS

Relative speed of sprockets is the same as for belt pulleys or sheaves.

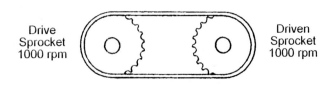

JDPX1628

Fig. 31 — Sprockets the Same Size

When two sprockets are the same size, they will rotate at the same speed (Fig. 31).

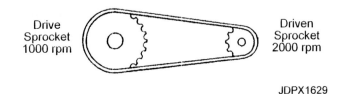

JDPX1629

Fig. 32 — Driven Sprocket Smaller than Drive Sprocket

If we keep the same *drive* sprocket, but use a smaller *driven* sprocket, the driven sprocket will turn faster (Fig. 32).

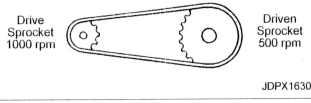

JDPX1630

Fig. 33 — Drive Sprocket Smaller than Driven Sprocket

If we use a smaller *drive* sprocket, but keep the *driven* sprocket the same, the driven sprocket will turn slower (Fig. 33).

Proper Direction of Chain Travel

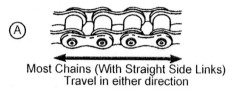

Most Chains (With Straight Side Links)
Travel in either direction

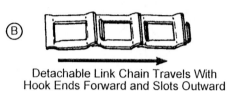

Detachable Link Chain Travels With
Hook Ends Forward and Slots Outward

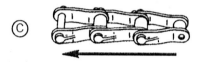

Pintle and H-Type Chains Travel With
Barrel Forward

JDPX1631

Fig. 34 — Proper Direction of Chain Travel

Chains must be operated in the proper direction to assure maximum wear life of both chain and sprockets. Follow the recommendations below to reduce wear on pin bearing surfaces, chain links, and sprocket teeth.

- Standard Roller Chains and Double-Pitch Roller Chains, with straight side links, travel in either direction (Fig. 34, A).

- Detachable Link Chains travel with hook ends forward and slots outward (Fig. 34, B). Otherwise, the bars wear excessively.

- Pintle and H-Type Chains should be operated with the barrel forward (Fig. 34, C).

Only for special speed-up or long center drives, should the chains in (B) and (C) be operated with the open end forward.

Practice Safe Maintenance

 CAUTION: Never attempt to adjust a chain while it is operating. Keep hands, feet, and clothing away.

The following safety precautions must be taken when performing chain drive inspections and maintenance.

- Always shut off the power to the drive and wait for all parts to stop moving before doing any maintenance work on power drives. Lock the controlling switch In the OFF position If possible.

- Make sure that the machine drive components are in a neutral position to avoid accidental movement or start up.

- Use caution while inspecting chains or sprockets to avoid being cut by burrs or sharply worn edges.

- Always replace shields if you must remove them to repair or adjust the chain drive.

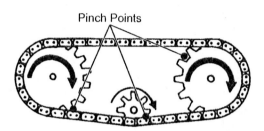

Chain Drive

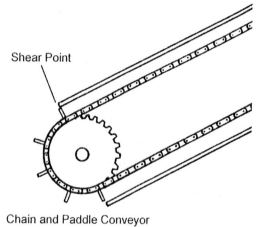

Chain and Paddle Conveyor

JDPX1632

Fig. 35 — Avoid Hazardous Pinch Points and Shear Points

- Avoid hazardous pinch points or shear points on the rotating parts of the chain drive (Fig. 35). Keep hands, feet, and clothing away from chain drives while in operation.

- Wear proper clothing when working around rotating components with potential wrap points. Never wear loose, bulky or ragged clothes around chain drives.

Starting and Stopping Chains

In general, avoid starting a chain which is under heavy load. Engage the chain drive SLOWLY and check for proper operation before putting it under full load.

CONVEYOR AND ELEVATOR CHAINS

These chains require special precautions for starting and stopping.

To avoid overloads, follow these steps:

1. Whenever possible, unload a conveyor or elevator before shutting it down. This allows a restart under no load and prevents a down-load from standing on the conveyor during shutdown.

2. Before start-up, check the surrounding area for obstructions that might overload the chain. Also before starting, or preferably after stopping, clean out any foreign material, especially the kind that "sets up" or hardens. Whenever possible, clean an elevator before starting it.

3. Start the chain and run it for a moment before applying a load. Check lubrication, and be sure all chain joints articulate freely.

4. Run chains periodically during shutdown periods to keep joints from binding or "freezing" and to reduce overloads when starting.

5. If the chain runs in excessive heat, start it before the temperature is elevated. When stopping, run until the heat has lowered to the normal range for a stationary chain.

Aligning Shafts and Sprockets

Proper alignment of sprockets and shafts is necessary for maximum wear life. Rapid wear will result from misalignment due to rubbing of chain parts against sides of sprocket teeth and excessive friction in the joints caused by racking and twisting.

To assure correct alignment, follow the following steps:

JDPX1633

Fig. 36 — Leveling Shafts Using A Machinist's Level

1. Carefully **level the shafts** if they are running on the same line. Use a machinist's level directly on the shafts (Fig. 36). With a multiple-width sprocket, a spirit level can be applied across the sprocket teeth.

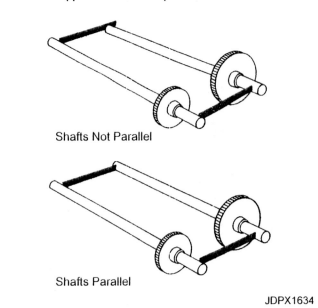

Shafts Not Parallel

Shafts Parallel

JDPX1634

Fig. 37 — Aligning Shafts For Parallelism Using A Feeler Bar

2. **Align the shafts**, using a feeler bar to see if they are parallel (Fig. 37). Recheck the level adjustment. Tighten all securing bolts and nuts to hold alignment.

JDPX1635

Fig. 38 — Aligning Sprockets Using a Straight Edge

3. **Align the sprockets** axially on the shafts, using a straight edge (Fig. 38). Take care to apply the straight edge to a finished surface on the side of the sprocket. For long center distances, a stretched wire can be used instead of a straight edge.

4. With a shaft having some end play (like the shaft of an electric motor), **align the sprockets with the shaft in its running position**. To determine the running position, chalk the shaft, run the motor at operating speed, and scribe a line in the chalk opposite a convenient fixed point. Adjust the alignment with the shaft blocked in this position.

5. **Secure each sprocket** to prevent axial end play by means of a setscrew, or by collars setscrewed to the shaft. However, do not depend on setscrews to prevent the sprockets from turning on the shaft ... keyways in the shaft are best.

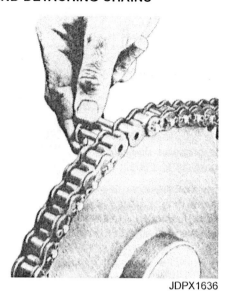

JDPX1636

Fig. 39 — Installing Roller Chain

To couple the ends of a chain:

1. Loosen the chain tighteners to provide sufficient "working slack."

2. Bring the chain ends together over one sprocket, using the sprocket teeth to hold the chain.

3. Insert the pin or pin link to couple the chain into an endless strand (Fig. 39).

4. Adjust the chain tighteners to provide the proper tension for operation.

The above method is especially useful for coupling drive chains.

When it is necessary to couple a chain in the span between the sprockets, draw the ends together with a block and tackle or other device. Then follow steps 3 and 4 above.

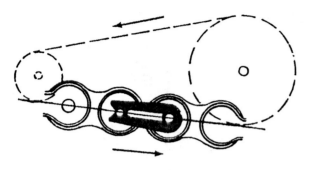

JDPX1637

Fig. 40 — Proper Master Link Clip Installation

NOTE: *When installing a chain using a master link clip (Fig. 40), the clip must be installed with the rounded (closed) end facing the direction of chain travel.*

To install an endless type chain without detaching the chain, either shorten the sprocket center distance until the chain can be placed over the sprockets or remove the sprockets from the drive and driven shafts. Position the chain on the sprockets, and install the chain and both sprockets at the same time.

Keep chain straight when coupling. Coupling a link when the chain is crooked may cause the chain to twist in operation.

Correct Method

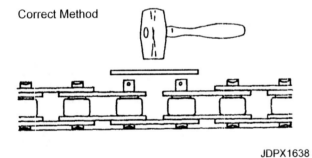

JDPX1638

Fig. 41 — Coupling Chains—Correct Method

To provide a solid back-up for the chain, assemble it in a straight line on a solid flat surface (Fig. 41), then feed the chain onto its drive.

Incorrect Method

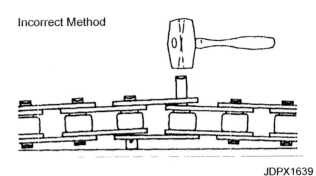

JDPX1639

Fig. 42 — Coupling Chains—Incorrect Method

For straight side bar chains, avoid driving the pin all the way through from one side (Fig. 42). Instead, assemble both pins in one side bar, insert in the chain, and then assemble the second side bar from the other side (Fig. 41).

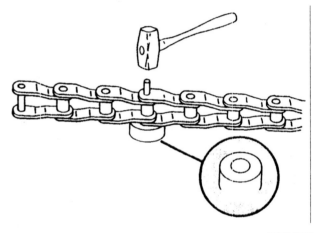

JDPX1792

Fig. 43 — Coupling Offset Side Bar Chains

When coupling offset side bar chains, support the lower side bar around the pitch hole with a block having a hole large enough to accommodate the pin end (Fig. 43). This will also prevent bending the side bars.

In most, chains there is a press fit between the pins and the side bar holes. To preserve this fit, couple and uncouple the chain as little as possible.

Do not weld pins in side bars. Instead, cotter or rivet the pin ends. In most cases, the press fit alone is sufficient to hold the pin in the side bar. If possible, use a straight coupler link rather than an offset one.

 CAUTION: Make sure all chain guards and shields are in place during operation.

Chain Detaching Tools for Roller Chains

The chain detacher is an inexpensive, convenient bench tool for uncoupling precision roller chain. It is designed to prevent damage to the chain during disassembly.

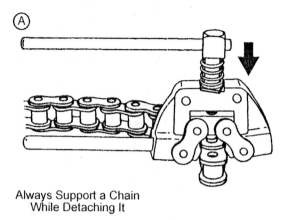

Always Support a Chain
While Detaching It

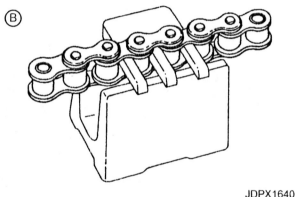

JDPX1640

Fig. 44 — Chain Detaching Tools for Roller Chain

In one type of chain detacher (Fig. 44, A), the chain is clamped into the fixture while a plunger is used to push the pin out.

Another type of chain detacher consists of two pieces; a fork and an anvil block (Fig. 44, B). The fork is slotted to fit the chain pitch and roller diameter and has tines of ample width to support the roller link side bars. The block and fork hold the chain in proper position, allowing the pins to be driven squarely out of the side bar.

Detachers are made for all popular sizes of roller chain and are readily available.

The best rule when detaching any chain is: *Support the chain while detaching it.*

Installing or Removing Detachable-Link Chains

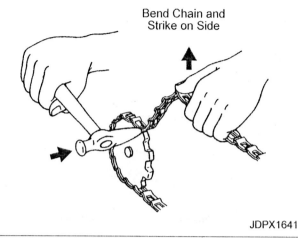

Bend Chain and
Strike on Side

JDPX1641

Fig. 45 — Detaching Detachable-Link Chain without Tool

To detach without a tool, bend the chain as shown in Fig. 45 and strike the side of the link to drive it out. The hook opening is slightly smaller than the side bar so a light hammer blow is needed to uncouple the links.

Couple the chain again in the same way. Be sure that the chain points in the proper direction shown in Fig. 34,(B).

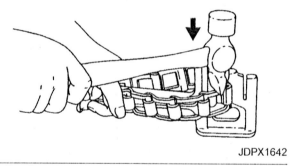

JDPX1642

Fig. 46 — Detaching Detachable-Link Chain with Tool

To detach using a tool (Fig. 46), place the chain in the slot as shown and strike the side of the link with a hammer.

Installing Conveyor Or Elevator Chains

Because of their length and weight, conveyor and elevator chains require special handling.

These chains are normally shipped coiled in segments. For elevators using a single strand of chain, couple the chain segments together and bolt the buckets to the attachments with the chain stretched out. This simplifies handling and installation and also helps keep the chain straight. Crooked or twisted chain can cause operating difficulties.

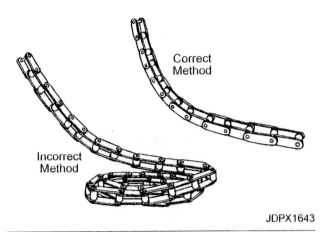

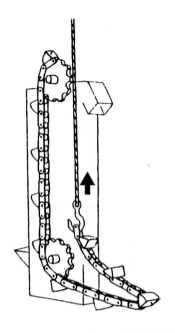

Fig. 47 — Feeding Chain onto Conveyors or Elevators

Do not feed the chain in on its side. Prevent the possibility of twist by feeding it in as shown in Fig. 47.

If the chain is twisted, straighten it by giving it a careful reverse twist with crowbars. Do this only while the chain is stretched out on the floor.

Fig. 49 — Installing Chain on Vertical Conveyors or Elevators

Another more common method is to feed the chain through one of the lower casing openings, hoisting it in place one end at a time (Fig. 49). This is done by hooking the chain several links back from one end. Slowly hoist the chain and place the short "free" end over the head sprocket. Secure the chain to prevent movement. Now hook the other end of the chain and hoist it into position as shown. Couple the two ends together at the head sprocket.

When replacing an elevator chain, uncouple the worn chain at the lower sprocket and attach the new chain. Thread the new chain into the elevator casing by carefully "jogging" the elevator drive or by pulling on the loose end of the old chain.

CHAIN SLACK

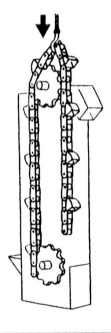

Fig. 48 — Installing Chain on Vertical Conveyors or Elevators

The quickest and easiest method for installing a vertical elevator chain is to lower it down over the head sprocket (Fig. 48). The chain ends are then coupled together at one of the lower casing openings. Adequate overhead space and hoisting equipment must be available for this method of installation.

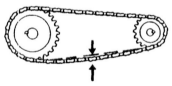

2% of Center Distance

JDPX1645

Fig. 50 — Correct Amount of Chain Slack

The correct amount of slack is essential for the proper operation of chain. Unlike belts, chain requires no initial tension and should **not** be tightened around the sprockets. Properly adjusted chain drives should permit slight flexing (by hand) in the slack strand of about 2 percent of the center distance (Fig. 50).

CHAINS TOO TIGHT

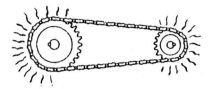

JDPX1646

Fig. 51 — Chain Too Tight, Binding

When a chain is *too tight*, the working parts carry a much heavier load than is necessary and work much harder without delivering any more power than properly installed chain. This causes rapid chain wear because of increased pressures in the joints (Fig. 51). In addition, this overloads and accelerates wear in the shaft bearings.

CHAINS TOO LOOSE

JDPX1647

Fig. 52 — Chain Too Loose, Whipping

Too much slack is also harmful. On long centers, particularly, too much slack will cause vibration and chain whipping, reducing the life of the chain (Fig. 52).

On long centers, the slack strand should be supported or taken up by idler sprockets or guides. The strip is simply a continuous support for the chain which prevents it from sagging too much.

HOW CHAINS "STRETCH"

The "stretch" a chain develops in service is due to material being worn off the pin and bushing bearing surfaces. After a period of operation, slack must be taken up to prevent the chain from jumping the sprockets.

All chain joint wear occurs when the chain is flexed over sprockets under load.

A chain adjusted with the proper amount of slack flexes only twice under load during each trip around the loop—once as the joint comes off the *driven* sprocket and again as it enters the *drive* sprocket.

When a chain is adjusted "fiddle string tight," wear is accelerated because each joint flexes four times under load as it travels around the chain loop.

HOW TO ADJUST CHAINS

For horizontal and inclined drives, the chain sag should be about 1/4 in. (6.35 mm) per 12 in. (305 mm) between shaft centers (with one side of the chain taut).

Vertical drives and those subject to shock loading, reversal or rotation should be adjusted so that both spans of the chain are almost taut.

For drives on fixed centers, chain tension is usually controlled by an adjustable chain tightener, either an idler sprocket or a shoe.

To determine the amount of sag, pull one side of the chain taut, allowing all the excess chain to accumulate in the opposite span.

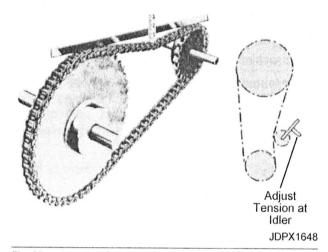

Adjust Tension at Idler

JDPX1648

Fig. 53 — Adjusting Chains

Place a straight edge over the slack span and pull the chain down at the center (Fig. 53). Measure the amount of sag from the top of the chain to the underside of the straight edge.

If necessary, adjust the shaft centers or the tightener to provide the manufacturer's recommended amount of sag for proper chain slack.

NOTE: On many sprockets—particularly cast ones—the teeth may not be perfectly concentric with the shaft. For this reason, be sure to turn the drive several times to recheck slack in all positions of the sprockets.

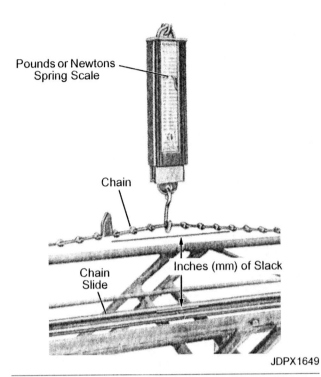

Pounds or Newtons Spring Scale

Chain

Chain Slide

Inches (mm) of Slack

JDPX1649

Fig. 54 — Checking Slack on Long Conveyor or Elevator Chains

On long chains for conveyers and elevators, slack is usually checked by pulling on the chain at the center of one side with a spring scale and measuring the slack at a recommended pounds (N) pull (Fig. 54).

Some long chains use automatic tighteners and do not require adjustment.

 CAUTION: Never attempt to adjust chains while they are operating.

ROLLER CHAIN "DON'TS"

- Never insert a new link in a chain that's been lengthened greatly by wear. The "bite" of the new link will be different and the resulting shock, each time the link engages the sprocket, will soon destroy the chain.

- Don't install a new chain on badly worn sprockets. A few hours of operation under such conditions will do more damage to the chain than months of normal use.

- Don't run chains too tight or too loose. Tight chains cause excessive loads on bearings. Loose chains cause noisy operation, chain pulsations or whipping and result in irregular sprocket speeds and abnormal wear.

- When installing a link, don't drive the connecting link plate down too far on the pins. This "squeezes" the chain joint so no oil can get down in between the link

plates, keeps joints from flexing and results in "whipping."

Maintenance of Chain Drives

Inspection of the chain drive on a regular basis may detect problem areas in time to prevent a major failure of the equipment. The following items should be checked during the periodic inspection.

Check for abnormal wear on the sides of the sprocket teeth and on the side bars which could indicate misalignment of the drive.

Chain elongation should be watched. A gradual increase in chain length is the result of normal wear. A sudden increase in chain slack indicates trouble in the drive.

Care should be taken to keep the chain and sprockets as clean as possible. Dirt or foreign material in the chain drive may cause unnecessary wear or even chain breakage.

The chain drive parts should be properly lubricated.

Cleaning Chains

Periodic cleaning is a good practice under even the best operating conditions. Follow these steps:

1. Remove chain from sprockets.

2. Wash chain in diesel fuel.

3. Dry chain with compressed air and soak chain in oil.

4. Hang chain to drain off excess lubricant.

5. Install chain.

NOTE: Use only kerosene or diesel fuel for cleaning an O-ring sealed drive chain. Any other cleaning solution may cause deterioration and swelling of the O-rings. Immediately blow the chain dry with compressed air after cleaning.

Storing Chains

STORING NEW CHAINS

Keep new chain in its box or wrapping. Store it indoors in a protected location, to keep grit and dirt out of the joints, and away from excessive heat or moisture, which destroys the initial factory lubrication.

Storing Chains On Idle Equipment

If equipment is to be idle for any length of time, protect chains from deterioration and prolong life as follows:

1. Clean thoroughly, and remove chain if possible.

2. Cover chain with heavy grease.

3. Wrap unmounted chain in heavy paper and store inside.

4. Apply a coating of grease to all finished surfaces of sprockets, and to any chain left mounted.

NOTE: *When placing equipment back into service, clean chains and sprockets of grease and lubricate thoroughly. Gummy storage lubricants cause excessive wear on chains and sprockets, and prevent the entry of fresh lubricant into the joints later on.*

Chains on elevators or conveyors which cannot easily be removed should be periodically run to prevent joints from "freezing" or binding and to reduce overloads when starting.

Lubricating Chains

There are four vital reasons for lubricating chains:

- **Reduce wear**

- **Protect against rust, corrosion, and heat**

- **Prevent seizing of pins and bushings**

- **Cushion shock loads**

Lubrication of chains is perhaps the most important factor in long service life. Running dry, exposed chains has been known to wear out chains in less than 200 hours. Manual lubrication can extend wear life three to ten times

 CAUTION: Never manually lubricate the chain while it is running.

Usually, SAE 30 or heavier oil is recommended for lubrication of the chain. The oil should be just light enough to penetrate the chain joints.

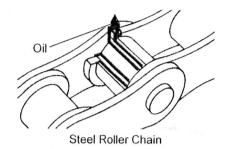

Steel Roller Chain

Detachable Link   Cast Pintle

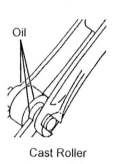

Combination   Cast Roller

JDPX1650

Fig. 55 — Lubrication Points on Chains

Oil application points on the chain slack side strand are usually best. Oil should always be applied to the side bar edges (Fig. 55) since access to the internal bearing surfaces of the chain is only possible through the clearances between the side bars or between the side bars and roller edges.

Dripping oil on the outside of the chain may not be enough. Oil must reach the vital bearing surfaces pointed out in top figure. To do this, oil must penetrate the gap between the inside and outside plates of roller chains. This can be achieved by oiling the chain while it is warm and then running it for a short time.

Chains which collect dirt and dust should still be oiled regularly. A "paste" of oil and dirt still wears less than a dry dirt packed chain joint.

NOTE: *For certain abrasive soil or sandy conditions, some manufacturers may not recommend lubrication of chains. However, this is the exception, not the rule.*

METHODS OF LUBRICATING CHAINS

Method of Lubrication	Manual		Semi-automatic	Automatic		
Application of Lubricant	Brush or oil can	Pressure lubrication	Drip Cup	Oil Bath	Oil Disk	Oil Stream
			Contact brush, direct drip	Chain dips into oil	Oil disk throws lube up on chain	Pump sprays oil on chain
Kind of Equipment	Conveyors, Elevators, Simple Drives	Conveyors	Conveyors and Elevators. Drives in low horsepower and speed range	Drives - low to moderate horsepower and speed	Drives - moderate to high horsepower and speed	Drives - high horsepower and speed

Methods of lubricating chains are:

Manual

- Oil can
- Brush
- Pressure (grease gun)

Semi-Automatic

- Drip cup

Automatic

- Oil bath
- Oil disk
- Oil stream

Notice that manual lubrication is adequate for most conveyors, elevators, and simple drives, while more complex drives with higher speeds and loads require more lubrication—some by automatic devices.

Here are some lubrication tips for the various methods:

Manual lubrication: Make sure that the lubrication schedule is being followed and that oil is being properly applied. (Usually with a brush or oil can just before the chain goes around a sprocket—apply every eight hours).

 CAUTION: Use the necessary safety precautions when lubricating chains. Never lubricate the chain while it is running.

Drip lubrication: Inspect the level of oiler cups and the rate of feed. Check that the feed pipes are not clogged.

Oil Bath or Disk systems: Inspect the oil level and check that there is no sludge.

Oil Stream systems: Inspect the oil level in the reservoir, check the pump drive and the delivery pressure so that there is no clogging of the piping or nozzles.

With reservoir systems, drain and refill per manufacturer's recommendations or at least once a year.

In general, oil viscosities should be the same as machine engines: Use heavier oils in hotter weather and lighter oils in colder weather.

Remember these six points about chain lubrication:

- Lubricate at regular intervals—even when chain collects dirt or dust.
- At higher speeds, lubricate more frequently.
- Remove excess dirt and dust from chains before lubricating.
- Lubricant must penetrate the chain joints. The lubricant should be applied to the side bar edges since access to the internal surfaces of the chain is only possible through clearances between the side bars or between the side bars and roller edges.
- Protect the chain from contaminants wherever possible.
- Follow the manufacturer's instructions on lubrication.

Chain Wear

Single-pitch chains should be replaced when wear elongation (stretch) equals 3 percent of the original chain length.

To determine chain wear, pull the used chain taut and measure the length of the chain. Compare this length with the length of a new chain.

For example, a 66-pitch strand of 3/4 inch-pitch (19 mm-pitch) roller chain has an original length, when new, of 49-1/2 in. (1257 mm). When the chain elongates to 51 in. (1295 mm), it is ready for replacement.

When wear elongation reaches 3 percent, the file-hard bearing surface on pins and bushings has worn away, and joint wear greatly accelerates, requiring frequent slack adjustment.

Single-pitch chain can be operated past the 3 percent point, but the relatively few extra service hours obtained will not compensate for the downtime required for frequent slack adjustment.

Some low-speed, lightly loaded drives use double-pitch chain. Since double-pitch chain has only half as many joints per foot (meter) as single-pitch chain, the pin and bushing bearing surfaces are worn through when wear elongation reaches 1 to 2 percent of original chain length. Consequently, the double-pitch chain is ready for replacement at 1 to 2 percent stretch.

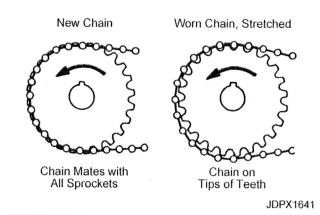

New Chain — Worn Chain, Stretched

Chain Mates with All Sprockets — Chain on Tips of Teeth

JDPX1641

Fig. 56 — Comparing New and Worn Roller Chains

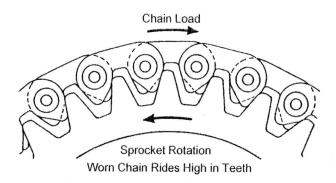

Chain Load

Sprocket Rotation
Worn Chain Rides High in Teeth

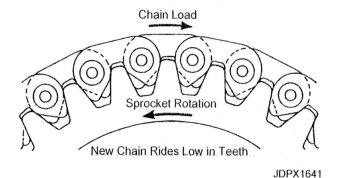

Chain Load

Sprocket Rotation

New Chain Rides Low in Teeth

JDPX1641

Fig. 57 — Comparing New and Worn Silent Chains

As chains wear and stretch, they do not mate properly with their sprocket teeth. Badly worn roller chains ride so far out of the tooth pockets that they may be off the working faces (Fig. 56).

Worn silent chains ride higher in the sprocket teeth as they wear (Fig. 57).

WEARING OF CHAIN PARTS

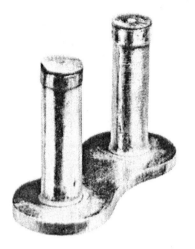

JDPX1659

Fig. 58 — Pin Wear (Lack of Lubrication)

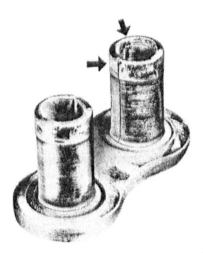

JDPX1660

Fig. 59 — Bushing Wear (Note Wear on Both Inside and Outside Diameters)

JDPX1661

Fig. 60 — Roller Wear

When chains are worn and do not fit their sprockets, the link entering the driven sprocket on the slack side will be on top of the sprocket tooth, and will jump a tooth, causing extremely high loads in the chain links. The abnormally high loads cause chain breakage and decrease the life of the drive.

The wear rate of a chain depends upon many factors, the most important of which is lubrication. Discolored pins (brown or black due to "burned oil") or red oxide (fretting) are sure signs that the chain joint has not received sufficient lubrication (Figs. 58, 59). A chain wears many times faster when run dry than when run well lubricated. Because a little oil greatly reduces the wear rate, wear will vary widely in the same chains. Two chains being compared rarely have exactly the same amount of oil reaching the joints.

Starved lubrication also causes some joints in the chain strand to wear more rapidly than others, which causes the chain to operate very roughly and makes it impossible to obtain the proper slack adjustment for the entire strand length.

Another factor known to influence chain joint wear is the "severity of environment." Abrasive material that can reach the chain joints will cause rapid wear. Even though chains operate in abrasives, lubrication can extend chain life. Corrosion also greatly accelerates pin and bushing wear.

The drive configuration also influences wear life of the chain. For example, in transmitting a given horsepower (kW) at a given rpm, the fewer the teeth in the sprocket, the greater the wear rate of the chain. Maintaining the correct amount of chain slack is also essential for obtaining maximum drive life. Finally, misaligned or worn sprockets are other factors that increase the wear rate of a chain drive, especially steel roller chain (Fig. 60).

Never insert new links in a chain that has been elongated by wear. The new links will have shorter pitches, causing shock when engaging the sprocket. This will soon destroy the chain.

IMPORTANT: Do not install a new chain on badly worn sprockets. More damage will occur to the chain in fewer hours than under months of normal use.

GALLING

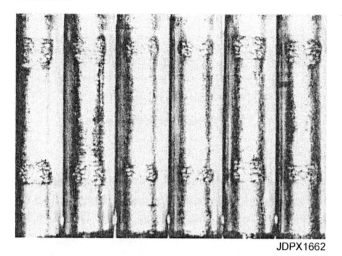

Fig. 61 — Galling of Chain Pins

Galling of bearing surfaces occurs when the mating surfaces weld. When a chain joint galls and the joint flexes over the sprockets, the weld breaks and tears chunks of metal out of the surface of the pin and bushing (Fig. 61). When galling occurs, "wear" is extremely rapid.

Galling always occurs because of lack of lubrication in the chain joints. On well-lubricated chains with hardened pins and bushings, operating within recommended speed limits, galling will not occur at loads up to the yield strength of the chain.

If chain speed is greater than that recommended, it is impossible to get lubrication into the chain joint, regardless of how much oil is put onto the chain. Under these conditions, galling will occur even though working chain tension is very low.

CHECKING WEAR ON CHAINS

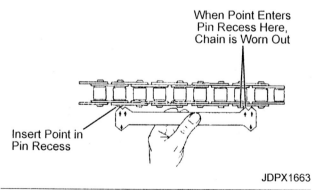

When Point Enters
Pin Recess Here,
Chain is Worn Out

Insert Point in
Pin Recess

JDPX1663

Fig. 62 — Using Special Gauge To Check Wear On Roller Chain

Special gauges are available to check wear on chains. The gauge shown in Fig. 62 indicates the chain is worn out when both points will enter pin recesses.

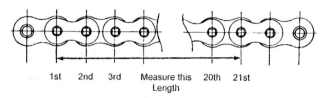

1st   2nd   3rd   Measure this   20th   21st
                     Length

JDPX1664

Fig. 63 — Measuring Chain Length

In some instances, a "new chain" standard length and an "old chain" wear limit length may be specified for a given number of chain links, rather than the total length of the chain. For example, the specified standard length for 20 links of new chain may be 15 inches (381 mm) and the wear limit length is 15-1/2 inches (393 mm).

Remember when measuring chain links that the number of pins will total one more than the number of links, i.e., 21 pins in 20 links (Fig. 63).

WEAR LIMITS ON ROLLER CHAINS

The chart below shows your typical wear limits on single-pitch roller chains. When the chain wears and "stretches" until it reaches the "old" length, it should normally be replaced.

Strand Length in Pitches	Chain Length in. (mm)							
	No. 40 Chain (08A)		No. 50 Chain (10A)		No. 60 Chain (12A)		No. 80 Chain (16A)	
	New	Old (Replace)	New	Old (Replace)	New	Old (Replace)	New	Old (Replace)
40P	20 (508)	20-5/8 (523)	25 (635)	25-3/4 (654)	30 (762)	31 (787)	40 (1016)	41-1/4 (1047)
50P	25 (635)	25-3/4 (654)	31-1/4 (793)	32-3/16 (817)	37-1/2 (952)	38-5/8 (981)	50 (1270)	51-1/2 (1308)
60P	30 (762)	30-7/8 (784)	37-1/2 (952)	38-5/8 (981)	45 (1143)	46-3/8 (1177)	60 (1524)	61-3/4 (1568)
70P	35 (889)	36 (914)	43-3/4 (1111)	45-1/16 (1144)	52-1/2 (1333)	54 (1371)	70 (1778)	72 (1828)
80P	40 (1016)	41-1/4 (1047)	50 (1270)	51-1/2 (1308)	60 (1524)	61-3/4 (1568)	80 (2032)	82-1/2 (2095)
90P	45 (1143)	46-3/8 (1177)	56-1/4 (1428)	58 (1473)	67-1/2 (1714)	69-1/2 (1765)	90 (2286)	92-3/4 (2355)
100P	50 (1270)	51-1/2 (1308)	62-1/2 (1587)	64-3/8 (1635)	75 (1905)	77-1/4 (1962)	100 (2540)	103 (2616)

CORROSION

Cadmium Plated Chain (Rusted)

Stainless Steel Chain (Rust Discoloration Only)

Stainless Steel Chain (No Rust)

Standard Chain (Badly Rusted)

JDPX1665

Fig. 64 — Corrosion Of Chains (Atmospheric Corrosion)

When a chain is subjected to corrosion in the field, its mechanical properties are impaired. There is usually a general roughening of the surface, such as pitting and the formation of rust (Fig. 64).

Chains Breaking

Link breakage is usually due to fatigue and may be caused by improper installation, underrating, excess vibration, the chain jumping the sprocket teeth resulting in severe and abnormal overloading, shafts out of parallel, or a foreign object entering between the chain and the sprocket tooth. A tensile breakage of the link may develop due to the same causes.

If tensile chain breakage does occur, it will usually be the pin. Such breakage generally develops due to overloading caused by the chain or sprocket becoming worn and the chain jumping the sprocket teeth. It may also be caused by shafts out of parallel or sprockets out of line.

Tight Joints

Fig. 65 — Tight Joints in Chain Strand

Tight joints, or stiffness of roller chain links (Fig. 65), generally result from the roller link bars moving off the ends of the bushings and rubbing against the pin link bars. This occurs most frequently at very high operating loads, and is accelerated by lack of lubrication. Chains are designed to resist this type of chain failure, and if it develops, it can be alleviated only by improving lubrication of the drive or by using larger chain.

Tight joints can also be caused by material between the chain parts, or by peening over the edges on the link bars from interference with an oversize hub on the sprocket, or by other obstructions in the chain path.

If a chain has become stiff because of material build-up in the joints, the chain should be thoroughly cleaned and relubricated. If this proves inadequate, an extra clearance chain should be considered.

If the stiffness results from peening on the link bars, the drive should be checked for alignment and obstructions.

If there is evidence of misalignment, i.e., wear on the inside of the link bars of the roller link, check the shaft and sprocket alignment. Misalignment may also be a factor in tight joints.

Sprocket Wear

Sprockets manufactured with the proper tooth form are essential for smooth drive operation and optimum chain service life.

If replacement chains give less service than the originals, check the sprockets for excessive wear.

Hooked Teeth

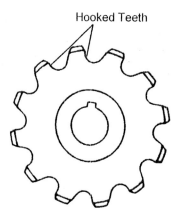

Fig. 66 — Worn Sprocket

Sprockets should be replaced when tooth wear progresses to a point where the teeth have a **hooked** appearance (Fig. 66).

The amount of sprocket tooth hooking a drive can tolerate before serious chain damage occurs varies with drive conditions. Generally, as sprocket speed and chain loading increase, the allowable amount of tooth hooking decreases. On exposed drives, sprockets with hardened teeth should last as long as three strands of chain.

If not too badly worn, sprockets can be reversed to allow the chain to engage the unworn face of the tooth. However, in many cases, the hub projection interferes with bearings or frame members, preventing sprocket reversal. Also use caution in reversing sprockets on high-speed drives. Do not reverse when the back sides of the teeth show any signs of wear.

When new sprockets are installed, they should be carefully aligned on the shafts with a straight edge. Misalignment increases drive noise and also increases chain and sprocket wear. Chains operating on misaligned sprockets have a tendency to develop tight joints because sprocket teeth force the inside plates outward on the bushings, thus binding the joint.

A worn sprocket in a misaligned drive will show abnormal wear on the **side** of its teeth.

Troubleshooting Chains

The following troubleshooting chart is designed to give a general guide to diagnosing problems with chains.

CHAINS TROUBLESHOOTING CHART		
Problem	**Possible Cause**	**Remedy**
Excessive Noise	Misalignment of sprockets	Check alignment and correct
	Too little or too much slack	Adjust centers for proper slack, or idler take-up
	Lack of lubrication	Lubricate properly... check lubricating mechanism to be sure oil is reaching working parts
	Loose casings or bearings	Draw up all bolts, and brace casings if necessary
	Chain or sprocket worn out	Replace chain and/or sprocket (some sprocket can be reversed)
	Chain pitch size too large	Check chain drive recommendation chart
	Insufficient number of teeth on sprockets or idler	Use sprockets with more teeth
Chain Climbs Sprockets	Poor fitting of chains on sprockets	Make sure sprocket bottom diameters are not oversize
	Chain worn out	Replace chain and sprockets (some sprockets can be reversed)
	Lack of chain wrap on sprocket	Revise drive arrangement to get more sprocket teeth in contact with chain, or use idler take-up to increase wrap
	Excessive chain slack	Adjust centers or take-up for proper slack
	Material build-up in sprocket tooth pockets	Remove material buildup ... protect drive from contact with foreign material, or use sprockets with mud relief, pitch line clearance.
Wear on chain side bars or link plates and sides of sprocket teeth	Misalignment	Remove chain and correct alignment of sprockets and shafts

CHAINS TROUBLESHOOTING CHART (CONTINUED)

Problem	Possible Cause	Remedy
Broken pins, bushings or rollers	Chain speed too high for pitch and sprocket size	Use shorter pitch chain of equivalent or greater strength and/or check number of sprocket teeth to be sure it is within recommended limits for speed involved. Select a sprocket with increased number of teeth, if necessary.
	Heavy shock or sudden loads	Reduce shock loads if possible (easy starts assure longer life).
	Material buildup in sprocket tooth pockets	Remove material build-up ... protect drive from contact with foreign material, or use sprockets with mud relief, pitch line clearance
	Lack of lubrication	Lubricate properly
	Chain or sprocket corrosion	Protect from corrosion with proper cleaning and lubrication
	Wrong or badly worn sprockets	Check sprockets for wear and correct bottom diameter.
Chain clings to sprockets	Wrong chain or badly worn sprockets	Replace chain and sprockets (some sprockets can be reversed)
	Heavy or tacky lubricant	Clean and lubricate properly
	Material buildup on drive sprocket tooth pockets	Remove material build-up ... protect drive from contact with foreign material, or use sprockets with mud relief, pitch line clearance.
Chain whips	Excessive chain slack	Install chain take-up or idler, or adjust centers
	High pulsating loads	Reduce load where possible or replace chain with one of suitable strength
	One or more stiff chain joints	Remove stiff links, or drive back on pins to provide proper clearance between side bars (also see "Chain gets stiff" on next page)
	Uneven chain wear	Replace chain
Chain surging (conveyor chains)	Chain too tight or too loose	Adjust for proper slack
	Chain tightener in wrong location	Relocate tightener
	Mechanical interference	Inspect for interference with chain
	Sprockets too small	Use larger sprockets. (Pulsations in chain are much less with larger sprockets.)
	Chain track worn	Replace chain track
	Lack of lubrication	Lubricate properly
	Frozen chain joints or rollers	Free or replace frozen parts
	Concentrated loading	Even out loading of conveyor

CHAINS TROUBLESHOOTING CHART (CONTINUED)

Problem	Possible Cause	Remedy
Chain gets stiff	Lack of lubrication	Remove chain if dirty or corroded ... clean and lubricate properly
	Corrosion	Protect chain from corrosion
	Excessive overloads	Reduce overloads
	Material buildup in chain joint	Protect chain with guard ... clean and lubricate more often
	Peening of side plate edges	Check for chain interference and correct
	Misalignment	Check sprocket and shaft alignment
Broken sprocket teeth	Obstructions of foreign material in chain guards	Check chain and sprocket clearances ... remove foreign material
	Excessive shock loads, especially with small, cast-iron sprockets	Reduce excessive shock loads, or use steel sprockets
	Chain climbing sprocket teeth	(See items "Chain climbs sprockets" on page 27)
Chain fasteners fail	Vibration	Reduce vibration
	Obstructions striking cotter pins	Eliminate obstruction, or tap ends back until cotter pin fits snugly against side bars, or use riveted chain
	Cotter pins not installed properly	Correct faulty installation (pins should be properly spread and drawn back snugly against side bar)
Chain drive runs too hot	Operating faster than recommended speed	Check drive for recommended maximum speed and type of lubrication used
	Lack of lubrication	Increase volume of oil and/or cool oil in reservoir
	Chain operating too fast for bath lubrication	Use oil stream system of lubrication
	Chain immersed too deeply in oil (bath-lubricated drive)	Adjust oil level to proper height
	Chain or shafts rubbing against an obstruction or seal dragging	Remove obstruction

Test Yourself

1. Match each of the statements below with either "belt drives" or "chain drives."

    a. Have less slippage.

    b. Stretch at a faster rate.

    c. Least damaged by oil and grease.

    d. Generally more flexible.

    e. Can operate at higher temperatures.

    f. Require initial tension when installed

2. Name the three basic jobs of chains.

3. What is *pitch* of roller chains?

4. On horizontal chain drives, should the tightener be on the bottom or the top?

5. True or false? "Standard roller chain can operate in either direction."

6. On detachable link chain, should the hook ends travel forward or to the rear?

7. A horizontal chain drive has 48 inches (1219 mm) between its shaft centers. How much chain sag should it have?

8. By looking at the mating on the sprocket teeth, how can you tell if the *roller chain* is badly worn?

9. How do the profiles of sprocket teeth change as they wear?

10. True or false? "In some applications timing belts and chains perform equally well.'

APPENDIX

Measurement Conversion Chart

Metric to English

LENGTH
1 millimeter = 0.03937 inches. in
1 meter = 3.281 feet. . . . . ft
1 kilometer = 0.621 miles .mi

AREA
$1 \text{ meter}^2 = 10.76 \text{ feet}^2$ . . . . .ft^2
1 hectare = 2.471 acres . . . . acre
   (hectare = 10,000 m^2)

MASS (WEIGHT)
1 kilogram = 2.205 pounds. . . . . lb
1 tonne (1000 kg) = 1.102 short ton . . . . .sh tn

VOLUME
$1 \text{ meter}^3 = 35.31 \text{ foot}^3$ . . . .ft^3
$1 \text{ meter}^3 = 1.308 \text{ yard}^3$. . . . . .yd^3
1 meter3 = 28.38 bushel. bu
1 liter = 0.02838 bushel . . . . bu
1 liter = 1.057 quart . . . . qt

PRESSURE
$1 \text{ kilopascal} = 0.145 \text{ pound/in}^2$. . . . . psi

STRESS
1 megapascal or
$1 \text{ newton/millimeter}^2 = 145 \text{ pound/in}^2$ . . . . psi
   ($1N/mm^2 = 1MPa$)

POWER
1 kilowatt = 1.341 horsepower (550 lb-ft/s) . . . . hp
   (1 watt = 1 N•m/sec)

ENERGY (WORK)
1 joule = 0.0009478 British Thermal Unit . . . . .BTU
   (1 J = 1 W s)

FORCE
1 newton = 0.2248 pounds force . . . . .lb force

TORQUE OR BENDING MOMENT
1 newton meter = 0.7376 foot-pound . . . . lb-ft

TEMPERATURE
$t_C = (t_F - 32)/1.8$

English To Metric

LENGTH
1 inch = 25.4 millimeters . . . . mm
1 foot = 0.3048 meters . . . . m
1 yard = 0.9144 meters . . . . m
1 mile = 1.608 kilometers . . . . .km

AREA
$1 \text{ foot}^2 = 0.0929 \text{ meter}^2$. . . . .$m^2$
1 acre = 0.4047 hectare . . . . ha
   (hectare = 10,000 m^2)

MASS (WEIGHT)
1 pound = 0.4535 kilograms . . . . kg
1 ton (2000 lb) = 0.9071 tonnes . . . . t

VOLUME
$1 \text{ foot}^3 = 0.02832 \text{ meter}^3$ . . . .m^3
$1 \text{ yard}^3 = 0.7646 \text{ meter}^3$ . . . .m^3
$1 \text{ bushel} = 0.03524 \text{ meter}^3$ . . . .m^3
1 bushel = 35.24 liter. L
1 quart = 0.9464 liter L
1 gallon = 3.785 liter L

PRESSURE
$1 \text{ pound/inch}^2 = 6.895 \text{ kilopascals}$. . . . . .kPa
$1 \text{ pound/inch}^2 = 0.06895 \text{ bars}$. bar

STRESS
1 pound/in^2 (psi) = 0.006895 megapascal . . . . MPa
                     or newton/mm^2 . . . . N/mm^2
   (1 N/mm^2 = 1 MPa)

POWER
1 horsepower (550 lb-ft/s) = 0.7457 kilowatt . . . . kW
   (1 watt = 1 N•m/s)

ENERGY (WORK)
1 British Thermal Unit = 1055 joules . . . . J
   (1 J = 1 W s)

FORCE
1 pound = 4.448 newtons . . . . .N

TORQUE OR BENDING MOMENT
1 pound-foot = 1.356 newton-meters . . . . .N•m

TEMPERATURE
$t_F = 1.8 \times t_C + 32$

Metric Fastener Torque Values

	4.8	8.8	9.8	10.9	12.9
Property Class and Head Markings					
Property Class and Nut Markings	5	10	10	12	

MIF (TS1163)

	Class 4.8				Class 8.8 or 9.8				Class 10.9				Class 12.9			
	Lubricated[a]		Dry[a]		Lubricated[a]		Dry[a]		Lubricated[a]		Dry[a]		Lubricated[a]		Dry[a]	
SIZE	N•m	lb-ft	N•m	lb-ft	N•m	lb-ft	N•m	lb-ft	N•m	lb-ft	N•m	lb-ft	N•m	lb-ft	N•m	lb-ft
M6	4.8	3.5	6	4.5	9	6.5	11	8.5	13	9.5	17	12	15	11.5	19	14.5
M8	12	8.5	15	11	22	16	28	20	32	24	40	30	37	28	47	35
M10	23	17	29	21	43	32	55	40	63	47	80	60	75	55	95	70
M12	40	29	50	37	75	55	95	70	110	80	140	105	130	95	165	120
M14	63	47	80	60	120	88	150	110	175	130	225	165	205	150	260	109
M16	100	73	125	92	190	140	240	175	275	200	350	225	320	240	400	300
M18	135	100	175	125	260	195	330	250	375	275	475	350	440	325	560	410
M20	190	140	240	180	375	275	475	350	530	400	675	500	625	460	800	580
M22	260	190	330	250	510	375	650	475	725	540	925	675	850	625	1075	800
M24	330	250	425	310	650	475	825	600	925	675	1150	850	1075	800	1350	1000
M27	490	360	625	450	950	700	1200	875	1350	1000	1700	1250	1600	1150	2000	1500
M30	675	490	850	625	1300	950	1650	1200	1850	1350	2300	1700	2150	1600	2700	2000
M33	900	675	1150	850	1750	1300	2200	1650	2500	1850	3150	2350	2900	2150	3700	2750
M36	1150	850	1450	1075	2250	1650	2850	2100	3200	2350	4050	3000	3750	2750	4750	3500

a. "Lubricated" means coated with a lubricant such as engine oil, or fasteners with phosphate and oil coatings. "Dry" means plain or zinc plated (yellow dichromate - Specification JDS117) without any lubrication.

DO NOT use these hand torque values if a different torque value or tightening procedure is given for a specific application. Torque values listed are for general use only and include a ±10% variance factor. Check tightness of fasteners periodically. DO NOT use air powered wrenches.

Shear bolts are designed to fail under predetermined loads. Always replace shear bolts with identical grade.

Fasteners should be replaced with the same class. Make sure fastener threads are clean and that you properly start thread engagement. This will prevent them from failing when tightening.

When bolt and nut combination fasteners are used, torque values should be applied to the NUT instead of the bolt head.

Tighten plastic insert or crimped steel-type lock nuts to approximately 50 percent of the dry torque shown in the chart, applied to the nut not to the bolt head. Tighten toothed or serrated-type lock nuts to the full torque value.

Reference: JDS-G200.

Metric Fastener Torque Values - Grade 7

NOTE: When bolting aluminum parts, tighten to 80% of torque specified in table.

Size	N•m	(lb-ft)
M6	9.5—12.2	(7—9)
M8	20.3—27.1	(15—20)
M10	47.5—54.2	(35—40)
M12	81.4—94.9	(60—70)
M14	128.8—146.4	(95—108)
M16	210.2—240	(155—177)

Inch Fastener Torque Values

SAE Grade and Head Markings	No Marks — 1 or 2[a]	5 5.1 5.2	8 8.2
SAE Grade and Nut Markings	No Marks — 2	5	8

MIF (TS1162)

	Grade 1				Grade 2[a]				Grade 5, 5.1 or 5.2				Grade 8 or 8.2			
	Lubricated[b]		Dry[b]		Lubricated[b]		Dry[b]		Lubricated[b]		Dry[b]		Lubricated[b]		Dry[b]	
SIZE	N·m	lb-ft	N·m	lb-ft	N·m	lb-ft	N·m	lb-ft	N·m	lb-ft	N·m	lb-ft	N·m	lb-ft	N·m	lb-ft
1/4	3.7	2.8	4.7	3.5	6	4.5	7.5	5.5	9.5	7	12	9	13.5	10	17	12.5
5/16	7.7	5.5	10	7	12	9	15	11	20	15	25	18	28	21	35	26
3/8	14	10	17	13	22	16	27	20	35	26	44	33	50	36	63	46
7/16	22	16	28	20	35	26	44	32	55	41	70	52	80	58	100	75
1/2	33	25	42	31	53	39	67	50	85	63	110	80	120	90	150	115
9/16	48	36	60	45	75	56	95	70	125	90	155	115	175	130	225	160
5/8	67	50	85	62	105	78	135	100	170	125	215	160	215	160	300	225
3/4	120	87	150	110	190	140	240	175	300	225	375	280	425	310	550	400
7/8	190	140	240	175	190	140	240	175	490	360	625	450	700	500	875	650
1	290	210	360	270	290	210	360	270	725	540	925	675	1050	750	1300	975
1-1/8	470	300	510	375	470	300	510	375	900	675	1150	850	1450	1075	1850	1350
1-1/4	570	425	725	530	570	425	725	530	1300	950	1650	1200	2050	1500	2600	1950
1-3/8	750	550	950	700	750	550	950	700	1700	1250	2150	1550	2700	2000	3400	2550
1-1/2	1000	725	1250	925	990	725	1250	930	2250	1650	2850	2100	3600	2650	4550	3350

a. "Grade 2" applies for hex cap screws (not hex bolts) up to 152 mm (6-in.) long. "Grade 1" applies for hex cap screws over 152 mm (6-in.) long, and for all other types of bolts and screws of any length.

b. "Lubricated" means coated with a lubricant such as engine oil, or fasteners with phosphate and oil coatings. "Dry" means plain or zinc plated (yellow dichromate - Specification JDS117) without any lubrication.

DO NOT use these hand torque values if a different torque value or tightening procedure is given for a specific application. Torque values listed are for general use only and include a ±10% variance factor. Check tightness of fasteners periodically. DO NOT use air powered wrenches.

Shear bolts are designed to fail under predetermined loads. Always replace shear bolts with identical grade.

Fasteners should be replaced with the same grade. Make sure fastener threads are clean and that you properly start thread engagement. This will prevent them from failing when tightening.

When bolt and nut combination fasteners are used, torque values should be applied to the NUT instead of the bolt head.

Tighten plastic insert or crimped steel-type lock nuts to approximately 50 percent of the dry torque shown in the chart, applied to the nut not to the bolt head. Tighten toothed or serrated-type lock nuts to the full torque value.

Reference: JDS-G200.

TEST YOURSELF ANSWERS

CHAPTER 1

1. Flat, round, V-belts and serpentine.

2. b — From the sides of the sheave groove.

3. False — The top of the V-belt stretches.

4. To keep the belt on the pulley.

5. The shaft for the driven pulley (6 in. [125.4 mm] dia.) will turn twice as fast.

6. Variable speed is obtained by changing the effective diameter of the sheave or sheaves during operation.

7. True.

8. False — Sheave misalignment should not exceed 1/16 in. (1.6 mm) per 12 in. (305 mm) of shaft center distance.

9. True.

10. Cause 1: Lack of belt tension.

    Cause 2: Overload.

11. False. Dressings may damage V-belts. Proper tension and correct loads are the major ways to prevent slipping.

12. Remove all tension from the belts during storage.

13. False — Serpentine belts always have an automatic tensioner.

14. Serpentine belts.

CHAPTER 2

1. a — Chain drives; b — Belt drives; c — Chain drives; d — Belt drives; e — Chain drives; f — Belt drives.

2. Transmitting power, converting motion, and timing or synchronizing.

3. Chain pitch is the distance between the centers of the rollers.

4. On the bottom.

5. True.

6. Forward.

7. One inch (25.4 mm). Chain sag should be about 1/4 in. (6.35 mm) per 12 in. (305 mm) between shaft centers.

8. A badly worn chain will ride up out of the tooth sprockets. This is because it has "stretched."

9. The teeth get a "hooked" appearance on their forward edges from wearing on the chain.

10. True.

INDEX